CHINESE INSTANT POT COOKBOOK

CHINESE
INSTANT POT
COOKBOOK

60 Quick and Easy
Classic Recipes

SHARON WONG

Photography by Darren Muir

ROCKRIDGE
PRESS

For general information on our other products and services or to obtain technical support, please contact our Customer Care Department within the United States at (866) 744-2665, or outside the United States at (510) 253-0500.

Rockridge Press publishes its books in a variety of electronic and print formats. Some content that appears in print may not be available in electronic books, and vice versa.

Interior and Cover Designer: Linda Snorina
Art Producer: Sue Bischofberger
Editor: Anna Pulley
Production Editor: Ruth Sakata Corley
Production Manager: Riley Hoffman

Photography © 2021 Darren Muir; food styling by Yolanda Muir.
Author photo courtesy of Jimmy Wong.
Illustration used under license from shutterstock.com

Cover: Shrimp and Asparagus Stir-Fry, page 86.

Paperback ISBN: 978-1-63807-927-9
eBook ISBN: 978-1-63807-744-2
R0

For my loving and supportive family,
Jimmy, Matthew, Brandon,
Mom, and Dad

CONTENTS

INTRODUCTION

I was born and raised in the San Francisco Bay Area by my parents, both of whom immigrated from China. If you have lived in or visited San Francisco, you know that, within less than 47 square miles, you can try different Chinese regional cuisines as well as international variations of Chinese food created by the Chinese diaspora. My family is Cantonese, so most of my inspiration for this cookbook comes from Chinese banquets, dim sum, and Cantonese-style home cooking. I also include some recipes inspired by dining out at restaurants specializing in foods from Hong Kong, Shanghai, and Taiwan.

My parents taught me how to cook Chinese food in the traditional ways, but I also learned to be flexible in my approach to cooking. When my younger son was diagnosed with severe allergies to egg, peanut, sesame, shellfish, tree nut, and other common ingredients in Chinese food, I had to think about how we could embrace our Chinese food heritage with food allergy–related limits.

When I make food in the Instant Pot, I try to make it as authentically as possible and adapt when necessary. Soups and stews are done in a fraction of the time in this appliance. On the other hand, such speedy cooking can quickly transform

stir-fries and steamed vegetables into mush! However, I discovered that it is possible to stir-fry and steam vegetables in the Instant Pot with very short cooking times and, in some cases, I take food out of the pot before it even reaches pressure.

Although it may seem like a lot of effort to use the Instant Pot to cook for 0 minutes to 1 minute, then wash the appliance and put it away, it's worthwhile when making two or three dishes in a row. I try to first squeeze in a recipe that involves minimal cleanup, then make something substantial in the pot. This opens up more meal possibilities for people who live in a dorm or studio and have limited kitchen space, who are traveling in an RV, who are renovating their kitchen, and so on.

A pressure cooker cooks food under high pressure, which raises the boiling point of water and, as a result, foods take less time to cook, which preserves the nutritional value of the ingredients. This time-saving feature of the Instant Pot means you can cook dishes that typically take hours in just a fraction of the time—which also means you can make Chinese food you might not normally have time to make, and modify recipes to suit your dietary and nutritional needs.

Traditional Chinese recipes are delicious because they use many ingredients and involve many steps to create complex flavors. I, however, adapted the recipes for the Instant Pot by simplifying the steps and using only minimal ingredients. I also chose recipes that include ingredients that can be purchased easily in Asian markets, well-stocked supermarkets, or online.

There are some Chinese recipes I will always make in the Instant Pot from now on because they're just better when pressure cooked. I love making Curry Oxtail Stew (page 54) in the Instant Pot because the meat is fall-off-the-bone tender due to the moist-heat cooking environment. Five-Spice Soy Tea Eggs (page 17) are seasoned and cooked perfectly in the Instant Pot. The taste of Chicken Stock with Ginger (page 32) is far superior to any store-bought chicken broth or stock.

Thank you for buying and reading my book; it's an honor for this stay-at-home mom and former educator to share my recipes with you. To view even more recipes and learn how to adapt them for food allergies, visit my blog NutFreeWok for allergy-aware Asian fare.

CHAPTER ONE

THE CHINESE KITCHEN

Making delicious Chinese-inspired food at home starts with having some essential Chinese ingredients on hand. In this chapter you'll learn what ingredients you need, as well as the proper cooking techniques—home-cooked Chinese dishes are mostly stir-fried, steamed, simmered, and braised. You'll also learn how to use your Instant Pot to adapt these dishes and see how doing so can save you time and energy and provide a nutritious way to cook and eat.

Curry Oxtail Stew, page 54

Chinese Cooking and the Instant Pot

In the Instant Pot, you can pressure cook a variety of Chinese-style dishes, including rice, steamed vegetables, stews, stir-fries, soups, and more. It also significantly reduces the time and energy expended while cooking, which is especially useful on days when you're in a hurry or don't want to heat up the kitchen. You can also use the Instant Pot as a flavor builder; to brown meats; sauté aromatics like garlic, ginger, and onions; and deglaze the delicious bits stuck to the pot with wine or broth to add more flavor.

SAUTÉING TO BUILD FLAVOR

Cooking ingredients with the Sauté function maximizes their flavor with minimal effort when pressure cooking with the Instant Pot. Sautéing aromatics such as garlic, ginger, and onions in oil infuses the oil with flavor and adds a bit of caramelization to them, which makes the foods pop with flavor and adds fragrance to the dish. Using the Sauté function to brown or sear meats helps seal in juices and creates a nice crust.

Make sure the meats or vegetables you'll sauté are as dry as possible before browning, or the excess moisture on them will steam the foods instead. After washing the vegetables, drain them in a colander or spin them in a salad spinner to remove excess moisture.

After sautéing meats or vegetables, it's a good idea to add some liquid to the pot to deglaze the liner and loosen any stuck or burnt bits of food before proceeding with pressure cooking the remaining ingredients. Deglazing flavors your cooking liquid, prevents your savory dishes from tasting too sweet, and helps you avoid receiving the dreaded "Burn" warning on your Instant Pot.

STEAMING

The Steam function brings the water to a boil as fast as possible and cooks foods at the highest temperature. When steaming in the Instant Pot, it's important to add at least 1 to 2 cups of water, to place foods on a trivet or wire rack or in a steamer basket for maximum steam circulation, and to avoid overcooking or burning foods.

Because steam cooks food directly with moist heat, meats will not taste dried out and vegetables will retain more vitamins than those that are boiled, as boiling leaches nutrients out of the food and into the cooking water.

Steaming in the Instant Pot is a great way to cook temperature- or time-sensitive foods, such as fish, shellfish, and soft vegetables. Some Instant Pot models do not seal during the Steam mode, which allows you quick access to remove the food from the pot when it's ready.

If your Instant Pot does seal during the Steam function, quick release the pressure as soon as the cook time's up. Alternatively, use the Sauté function to boil water and steam food with a glass lid on the pot for easy access to your food when it's done.

I like my steamed vegetables to be crisp-tender and my seafood not to be overcooked, so I usually set my timer for the shorter end of the suggested cooking ranges and check it as soon as possible, then steam longer, if needed.

INSTANT COOKING IN ZERO TIME

Some models of Instant Pot allow you to set the timer to 0 minutes, which lets you pressure cook or steam a quick-cooking vegetable or seafood, or reheat a small amount of food in the shortest amount of time possible.

When you set the timer to 0 minutes, the Instant Pot will switch to the Keep Warm function once it reaches pressure and seals. With some foods, such as certain seafood items, you will want to remove the food from the pot immediately, but other foods can stay there for a few minutes more to cook in the residual heat.

Because this method is for quick-cooking foods, it's important to remove the food from the pot as soon as it's ready. If you don't want to watch the Instant Pot closely, set another timer for 5 minutes, which is an estimated amount of time it takes for the Instant Pot to build pressure for a small amount of food.

Some Instant Pot models do not allow setting the timer for 0 minutes; in that case, set the timer for 1 minute and take the food out once the pot reaches pressure.

MAKING DEEPLY FLAVORFUL STOCKS

Compared to stovetop cooking methods, the Instant Pot makes delicious stocks in a fraction of the time. Instead of simmering for hours, you can make a rich and flavorful stock in 2 to 3 hours, or you can make the stock, then allow the pot to release pressure naturally, and the Instant Pot will keep the stock warm for up to 10 hours, so it's ready to use when you need it.

If your Instant Pot has a Soup button, the pot is programmed for a gentle cook, so your soup stock remains clear. If you don't have a Soup button, pressure cook the stock on low pressure for 60 to 120 minutes. Or, if you are not in a hurry, use the slow cooker setting to make the broth in 4 to 10 hours.

One key technique to making Chinese-style stocks is to parboil the raw beef, pork, or bones before making the stock. You can use the Sauté function to boil half a pot of water, add the meat or bones, and parboil for 5 to 10 minutes. Drain the ingredients in a colander and rinse with cold water. This helps remove some of their impurities, ensuring you have a clearer broth and soup. Alternatively, parboil the meat or bones in a pot on the stovetop.

BRAISING AND STEWING

Preparing a large cut of meat with more conventional cooking methods can take a long time, especially when making a braise or stew, which requires cooking tougher cuts of meat on low heat for several hours. The difference between a braise and a stew is that meats cooked in a braise are partially submerged in a flavorful cooking liquid; in a stew, the meat is fully submerged in the liquid and often cooked with vegetables, which become part of the liquid.

Instant Pot braising or stewing takes about one-third of the time of stovetop cooking and one-tenth the time of a slow cooker, which allow you more flexibility about when to start cooking and what to do with your free time! And the results are just as flavorful.

On days with busy afternoons, I set up my Instant Pot earlier in the day. When the food is done cooking, the Instant Pot naturally releases the pressure and keeps the food warm until we are ready to eat.

SIMMERING TO FINISH COOKING

When the timer sounds at the end of a pressure cook cycle, the food continues to cook while under pressure and will continue to simmer and bubble for a few minutes after you remove the lid. This allows you to add some quick-cooking ingredients, such as scallions or other vegetables, to finish the dish. In some cases, you might want to use the Sauté function to simmer the sauce so it can evaporate a bit and thicken. You can also add a cornstarch slurry to thicken a sauce.

POT-IN-POT

You can cook foods in a pot inside the Instant Pot. This pot-in-pot method allows you to cook two dishes with similar cooking times at the same time in the Instant Pot, or cook sides, like rice or vegetables, to be served as part of a meal.

The recipes in this book were tested using stainless-steel containers because stainless steel is pressure-safe and conducts heat well, whereas other materials, such as glass and silicone, are more insulating. Allow extra time if you use glass or silicone containers.

It's important to use a trivet or wire rack to elevate the dish for even cooking. The Steam function heats the water as fast as possible and some water will evaporate, so be sure to add the amount of water specified in the recipe. Place the food in a separate pressure-safe vessel with a spoonful of water.

When it's done cooking, use silicone gloves, a plate lifter, or a sling to lift the dish out of the Instant Pot before serving.

ADAPTING STIR-FRY FLAVORS (AND MORE) TO THE INSTANT POT

It's possible to make a stir-fry in the Instant Pot using the Sauté function to stir-fry the ingredients in small amounts and then combine them in a sauce. It might take a little longer to cook the meal than on the stovetop, but the result is just as tasty.

One way to make a stir-fry is to first brown the chicken, meat, or seafood for flavor, then deglaze the pot to prevent a "Burn" warning. Then, add your fast-cooking foods last so they don't overcook during sautéing or pressure cooking.

The Flavors of Chinese Cuisine

As I learned from my mom, it's very simple to make Chinese food when you know basic techniques to build flavor, cook the ingredients just enough so they are neither undercooked nor overcooked, and mix and match favorite flavors with available and seasonal ingredients.

Douchi: Chinese fermented and salted black beans, called douchi, are made from black soybeans. Douchi is added first to the hot oil and stir-fried until fragrant, before other ingredients go into the pot. This technique adds pungency and umami to a dish.

Garlic, ginger, and scallions: Garlic, ginger, and scallions are the trinity of Chinese cooking and can be found in almost every Chinese recipe. They're fresh, flavorful ingredients with antiviral and anti-inflammatory health benefits.

Red cooking: Red cooking refers to two similar braising techniques that use a combination of light and dark soy sauces, rice wine, rock sugar, Chinese five-spice powder, and other ingredients to make a reddish braise. One technique involves sautéing garlic, ginger, and/or fermented bean curd in oil until fragrant and adding soy sauce and rice wine to braise meat. The other technique calls for simmering poultry or meat in soy sauce, rock sugar, and spices. The resulting sauce is often saved and reused as a master sauce.

Spicy: Chinese cuisine offers many ways to add heat to foods using fresh or dried chiles, hot sauces, or chili oil. Sichuan-style dishes often use Sichuan peppercorns, which are not only hot and spicy, but can also cause a numbing or tingling effect in one's mouth.

Stir-fry sauces and oils: Almost every stir-fry in this book is marinated with soy sauce, oyster sauce, sugar, and cornstarch. If you can't have corn, tapioca starch is a good substitute for cornstarch. You could also add minced garlic, white pepper, sesame oil, or chili oil for flavor variations.

Sweet-and-sour flavors: Lemon, orange, and sweet-and-sour sauce are familiar flavors in Chinese cooking, but there are many other ways to enjoy sweet-and-sour flavors in Chinese foods, such as by adding a small amount of sugar and vinegar to a cornstarch slurry or dipping savory dumplings into black vinegar. Making sweet-and-sour pickled vegetables, often added to dishes to balance rich or salty foods, or served as appetizers, is also a way to preserve vegetables for later use.

Ingredients for Instant Cooking

Making Chinese food at home starts with having the right ingredients on hand. If you had to pick three ingredients to start with, I'd recommend soy sauce, oyster sauce, and sesame oil. But, if you want to expand your repertoire, consider adding these core pantry staples, which will be used repeatedly throughout this book.

PANTRY INGREDIENTS

These staples are easy to find and relatively inexpensive at well-stocked supermarkets, and they keep well either in your cupboard or refrigerator.

Chili oil: Chili oil is made from hot oil poured into a mixture of different types of chili pepper flakes, aromatics, and, sometimes, Sichuan peppercorns to add flavor and heat. Refrigerate opened jars.

Chinese five-spice powder: Five-spice powder is a classic combination of different spices used in Chinese cooking. Despite its name, there can be up to 13 different spices in a five-spice mix. You can find five-spice powder in the spice section at your local supermarket or online.

Chinese rice wines: Also known as *mijiu*, rice wines are made from fermented glutinous rice and a small amount of wheat. I like to use a clear rice wine, which has a mild flavor. Shaoxing wine is a well-known, amber-colored rice wine with added spices. Huangjiu is a reddish rice wine made with red yeast. Meigui lujiu is a fermented sorghum rice wine with a rose infusion. Chinese rice wines are suitable for drinking unless they contain salt as a preservative. Refrigerate opened bottles.

Douchi: These salty, fermented black soybeans are dry but still soft and a little moist, with flecks of salt clinging to them. Once opened, store douchi in an airtight container at room temperature.

Dry sherry: This product is a suitable substitute for Chinese rice wine. You can also use mirin or sake, or whiskey, brandy, or wine, because what tastes good to you as a beverage will taste good in your food.

Garlic and black bean sauce: This jarred sauce is made from fermented black soybeans and garlic, soy sauce, and other seasonings. Refrigerate opened jars.

Hoisin sauce: This thick, dark-brown sauce is made from fermented soybean paste and can be used as a dip, glaze, or marinade. Hoisin sauce is salty and sweet, with a hint of spiciness. Gluten-free options are available. Refrigerate opened jars or bottles.

Oyster sauce: Oyster sauce is a brown viscous sauce made from the liquid that results from cooking oysters. It's delicious as a dip for blanched Chinese vegetables, and a small amount in Chinese stews or stir-fries adds a touch of sweetness and balance. Gluten-free and vegan (mushroom) options are available. Refrigerate opened bottles.

Rice: Unless otherwise indicated, I use medium-grain Calrose white rice in my recipes. Long-grain rice and jasmine rice are also popular options that can be used interchangeably. Buy one-pound bags of different varieties and follow the package instructions to cook it to find what you like.

Rice vinegar: Rice vinegar is made from rice wine, which is why it's sometimes called rice wine vinegar, but it should not be confused with rice wine, which has alcohol. If you are gluten-free, look for rice vinegar varieties that are labeled gluten-free (but always check the ingredients to be sure).

Sesame oil: Add toasted sesame oil at the end of cooking, or to dips, for its nut-like fragrance. Do not use it to sauté foods. If allergic to sesame, omit the sesame oil or try roasted sunflower seed butter in its place. Refrigerate opened bottles.

Soy sauce: Soy sauce is a liquid extract made from water, fermented soybean paste, wheat, and salt. The long fermentation process breaks down the soybean protein into amino acids, which are rich in umami flavors; the starches are broken down into sugars. Naturally brewed soy sauce tastes best. If the ingredient label includes hydrolyzed soy protein, caramel, and corn syrup, that indicates the soy sauce was chemically extracted and not naturally brewed. **Dark soy sauce**, sometimes referred to as thick soy sauce, is used for red cooked dishes and is added for color and sweetness. **Light soy sauce**, also referred to as thin soy sauce, is the most commonly used type, and is an all-purpose sauce. Light soy sauce adds flavor and saltiness to a dish. People who are watching their sodium intake may use a **low-sodium soy sauce** instead. If you use a low-sodium soy sauce, refrigerate it after opening and check the expiration date.

Tamari sauce: If you need a gluten-free soy sauce, look for tamari that's labeled gluten-free. Tamari is a type of Japanese soy sauce that's brewed with little to no wheat.

White pepper: White pepper has a fresh, spicy flavor that gives Chinese food a unique flavor. White pepper is from the same plant as black pepper, but white pepper is processed differently. If you can't find white pepper, use black pepper.

THE MAGIC OF UMAMI

Umami is a Japanese term that means "essence of deliciousness" and best describes foods that are savory, such as broths, cooked meat, and fermented foods. You can taste umami in foods that have high levels of naturally occurring amino acids, such as glutamate, as in seafood or vegetables.

Using Chinese sauces that are fermented, such as soy sauce, or that contain seafood, such as oyster sauce, is an easy way to add delicious savory flavors to your dishes because they are high in glutamates. People with a soy allergy can make a soy-free soy sauce using other umami-rich foods, such as beef broth, kelp, mushrooms, and other ingredients.

Adding shiitake and other types of mushrooms to a vegetarian dish will boost the umami flavor because mushrooms are high in glutamates. If desired, replace soy sauce and oyster sauce with mushroom soy sauce and mushroom oyster sauce.

Focusing on creating umami flavors is especially helpful for people on a low-sodium diet because umami foods naturally make food taste more delicious without added salt.

FRESH INGREDIENTS

There are too many varieties of Chinese vegetables to cover here. Check the recipe headnotes and tips for more information about Chinese vegetables. Some of my favorite ingredients that are essential to many Chinese-style recipes include:

Cilantro: Cilantro is one of a few fresh green herbs used in Chinese cooking. When used as a garnish, the heat from a dish wilts the cilantro slightly, which releases its fragrance.

Garlic: Garlic is used in many Chinese-inspired dishes. A little minced garlic can go into a sauce, or deep-fried slices can be used as a crunchy topping. Use the flat side of a chef's knife to smash the garlic to remove the peel easily.

Ginger: Fresh ginger is a tan-colored root with a thin skin. Ginger adds a fresh, zesty, hot, and spicy taste to Chinese foods. It's also good for digestion and high in antioxidants for good health. Select pieces for cooking that look heavy and smooth with a papery skin. You can use it peeled or unpeeled, but wash off any dirt between the knobs.

Mushrooms: Shiitake mushrooms are used in braises and stews. Fresh shiitake mushrooms require less preparation, but the flavor of dried shiitake mushrooms is worth the effort. Rinse dried shiitake mushrooms in water, then soak them in water for at least 30 minutes until soft. Reserve the soaking water to use as a cooking liquid.

Onions: I like to use sweet onions for most of my cooking, as they're mild flavored. Red onions, which are good raw, are also great lightly cooked in a stir-fry, and they add a pop of color to the dish. Deep-fried shallots make a great crunchy topping.

About the Recipes

The following chapters include a variety of popular Chinese dishes and flavors as well as some easy dishes to make for everyday meals at home. I tested the recipes in a 6-quart Instant Pot Duo and a 6-quart Instant Pot Pro. If you have a different size Instant Pot, you might need to adjust the amount of ingredients for the recipe so the Instant Pot is not more than two-thirds full.

Each recipe features the total prep and cooking times so you can accurately plan your meals, and includes the time the pot takes to come to pressure, the time cooked under pressure, and, if needed, the time it takes to release pressure naturally. Actual times may vary according to the temperature of the ingredients when they are put into the pot and the wattage of your Instant Pot.

When using the Sauté function, unless otherwise indicated, select medium heat.

Recipes also include dietary labels to help you quickly find those most suitable for you. All the recipes in this cookbook are peanut- and tree nut–free, as well as dairy-free. I use the following labels when applicable:

Gluten-Free: Recipes free of wheat, rye, or barley.

Soy-Free: Recipes free of soy and soy products. In other recipes that use soy sauce, you can use coconut aminos instead, but it is sweeter than soy sauce, so I recommend reducing sugar elsewhere in the recipe and adding some umami ingredients.

Super Fast: These dishes can be prepped and ready to serve in 30 minutes or less.

Vegan: Recipes free of animal products and by-products, including dairy, eggs, and honey.

Vegetarian: Recipes free of meat, poultry, and seafood.

INSTANT POT: OLD VERSUS NEW MODELS

The recipes in this book were tested in an Instant Pot Duo and an Instant Pot Pro. There are a few differences between the models, which might affect the recipe directions and the timing of the recipes. One major difference is whether the lid automatically closes the steam valve when you lock it. Older models have a knob that you must turn to seal the valve and again to release the pressure, whereas newer auto-seal lids have an easy steam release switch.

Another difference between the models is whether the Pressure Cook function is labeled with a Manual button or a Pressure Cook button. With older models, after you select the function and time, the Instant Pot starts automatically, but with the newer models, you must also select the Start function. Older models have a simple control panel to adjust any settings, such as by pressing the + or – buttons, whereas some of the newer models have a dial and words on the screen to select high or low pressure. Note that when the recipe instructions don't mention a specific program to pressure cook, select the default Manual or Pressure Cook button.

Some models have a Steam function, and others do not. The Instant Pot Pro has a Steam function but does not build pressure or seal, which seems to require more time than pressure cooking. Because pressure cooking is, essentially, cooking with steam and not all models have a Steam function, I use the Pressure Cook function for consistent results.

Instant Pot models vary in wattage from 1,000 watts to 1,400 watts, depending on the model and size. Models with a higher wattage will cook faster than ones with a lower wattage. This difference will have a slight impact on how long it takes to reach pressure and seal.

Recipe tips include:

Ingredient tip: More information about an ingredient, how to shop for it, or other ways to use it. In some cases, there are vegetarian or other substitutions for certain ingredients.

Prep tip: Information on how to prep an ingredient, how to save time, and make-ahead options.

Variation: Suggestions for adapting recipes for gluten-free and vegetarian options, or using a different type of meat, poultry, or seafood than what is specified.

ADAPTING RECIPES TO HIGH ALTITUDES

At sea level, the boiling point of water is 212°F (100°C), and with a pressure cooker, the boiling point of water can increase to 250°F (121°C). Pressure cookers cook at high pressure, which raises the boiling point of water. As a result, pressure-cooked foods are cooked at a higher temperature and require less time to finish cooking.

Because the air pressure is slightly lower at high elevations, water boils at a lower temperature, which is why it takes longer to cook. At 2,000 feet, the boiling point of water is 208.4°F (98°C) and at 10,000 feet, it is 193.6°F (90°C), which can substantially alter cooking times.

Using an Instant Pot can speed the cooking process by raising the boiling point of water, but your elevation might affect how much faster it reaches that point. The general rule is for every 1,000 feet above 2,000 feet, increase cooking times by 5 percent. For example, at 3,000 feet, increase the cooking time by 5 percent; at 4,000 feet, increase the cooking time by 10 percent; at 5,000 feet, increase the cooking time by 15 percent, etc.

Results may vary. Write down the extra minutes needed and your results, so you can refine your estimated times in the future.

APPETIZERS

Wontons with Chicken and Pork Stock, page 26

SHUI ZHENG DAN (WATER-STEAMED EGG)

Shui zheng dan translates to "water-steamed egg." It's a simple dish with lightly beaten eggs gently stirred together with water or broth for more flavor, then steamed until silkier than soft tofu. Pressure cook this dish in an aluminum foil–wrapped 2- to 4-cup stainless-steel bowl.

SERVES 4

PREP TIME:
5 minutes

PRESSURE BUILD:
5 minutes

PRESSURE COOK:
10 minutes, high

PRESSURE RELEASE:
Quick

TOTAL TIME:
20 minutes

1 cup water

2 large eggs

1 cup chicken broth or water

1 scallion, white and green parts, thinly sliced (optional)

1 teaspoon oyster sauce or light soy sauce

1 teaspoon sesame oil

1. Pour the water into the Instant Pot and place a trivet inside.

2. In a 4-cup pressure-safe bowl, lightly beat the eggs. Gently stir in the broth to avoid adding air bubbles into the egg. If you don't like raw scallion as a garnish, add the chopped scallion (if using) to the egg mixture.

3. Wrap the bowl with aluminum foil and lower the bowl onto the trivet.

4. Lock the lid. Program to pressure cook for 10 minutes on high pressure.

5. When the timer sounds, quick release the pressure. Carefully remove the lid and take the steamed eggs out of the pot.

6. Drizzle with oyster sauce and sesame oil and sprinkle with the raw scallion (if using, and you did not already add it).

VARIATION: If you have Chinese dried seafood, such as small, dried shrimp or dried scallops, add them in step 2 for more umami flavor. Rinse and soak the dried shrimp in water for a few minutes. If using dried scallops, rinse one, break it into 10 to 12 small pieces, and soak in water for a few minutes. Reserve the soaking water for the recipe and use it in place of some of the broth.

FIVE-SPICE SOY TEA EGGS

Making a soy sauce and tea brine with Chinese five-spice powder allows the flavors to seep through the cracked eggshells, revealing a beautiful design on the egg whites. The eggs make a great appetizer or snack after soaking in the hot brine. If you love tea eggs and want to make more for a crowd, you can cook up to 12 eggs at a time.

MAKES 6 EGGS

PREP TIME:
10 minutes, plus 30 minutes to soak

PRESSURE BUILD:
10 minutes

PRESSURE COOK:
5 minutes, high

PRESSURE RELEASE:
Quick

TOTAL TIME:
55 minutes

2 cups water

¼ cup light soy sauce

2 tablespoons sugar

1 tablespoon rice wine

2 teaspoons oolong tea, or 2 black tea bags

1 teaspoon Chinese five-spice powder

1 (1-inch) piece fresh ginger, thinly sliced

½ teaspoon salt

6 large eggs

1. In the Instant Pot, combine the water, soy sauce, sugar, wine, tea, five-spice powder, ginger, and salt. Place a steamer basket or a trivet inside and arrange the eggs in it.

2. Lock the lid. Program to Steam or Egg for 5 minutes on high pressure. While the eggs cook, prepare an ice bath.

3. When the timer sounds, quick release the pressure and carefully remove the lid. Using a slotted spoon, transfer the eggs to the ice bath.

4. Gently tap the eggs on a hard surface to create small cracks in the shells, but not so hard that the eggshells fall apart.

5. Transfer the brine to a heatproof container, add the eggs, and let soak for at least 30 minutes before serving.

6. Refrigerate any leftover eggs in the brine overnight, covered, and discard the brine the next day.

VARIATION: Five-spice soy peanuts are also cooked with similar ingredients and then soaked in a brine until ready to eat. Soak and rinse raw, in-the-shell peanuts a few times to remove any dirt. Omit the tea, increase the salt and five-spice powder to 2 teaspoons each, add enough water to cover the peanuts, and weigh the peanuts down with a trivet. Pressure cook for 30 minutes and use a natural pressure release for 20 minutes. Let the peanuts soak in the brine until the liquid cools to room temperature, or overnight.

SWEET-AND-TANGY CHICKEN PINEAPPLE MEATBALLS

I love heat-and-serve pineapple and chicken meatballs for an appetizer or a quick meal. I've adapted my oven-baked recipe for the Instant Pot and use ground chicken to save time. This recipe also makes a sweet-and-tangy sauce.

SERVES 4

PREP TIME:
15 minutes, plus 15 minutes to chill

SAUTÉ:
20 minutes

PRESSURE BUILD:
10 minutes

PRESSURE COOK:
2 minutes, high

PRESSURE RELEASE:
Quick

TOTAL TIME:
1 hour 2 minutes

1 pound ground chicken

1 (8-ounce) can crushed pineapple, drained, juice reserved, divided

½ cup panko bread crumbs

1 large egg, lightly beaten

4 teaspoons cornstarch, divided

4 teaspoons light soy sauce, divided

1 tablespoon dried chives or parsley

1 teaspoon garlic powder

1 teaspoon grated fresh ginger

1 teaspoon onion powder

½ teaspoon salt

4 teaspoons neutral oil, divided

1 tablespoon honey

1. Line a rimmed baking sheet with parchment paper.

2. In a medium bowl, combine the ground chicken, ¼ cup of crushed pineapple, panko, egg, 2 teaspoons of cornstarch, 2 teaspoons of soy sauce, chives, garlic powder, ginger, onion powder, and salt. Stir vigorously for about 5 minutes until the mixture forms a paste.

3. Shape 1 heaping tablespoon of chicken mixture into a meatball and place on the lined baking sheet. Repeat with the remaining chicken mixture and roll 16 meatballs total. Cover with plastic wrap and refrigerate for at least 15 minutes, or overnight.

4. On the Instant Pot, select Sauté and preheat the pot.

5. Once hot, pour in 2 teaspoons of oil and add half the meatballs. Brown for 4 minutes, flip the meatballs, and brown for 5 minutes more. Transfer the browned meatballs to a plate. Pour in the remaining 2 teaspoons of oil and add the remaining meatballs. Brown as directed for the first batch. Transfer the browned meatballs to the plate with the first batch.

6. Add ½ cup of the reserved pineapple juice to the pot to deglaze, scraping up any browned bits from the bottom.

7. Return the meatballs to the pot and lock the lid. Program to pressure cook for 2 minutes on high pressure.

8. In a small bowl, whisk the remaining 2 teaspoons of cornstarch, 2 tablespoons of pineapple juice, remaining 2 teaspoons of soy sauce, and honey until smooth. Set aside.

9. When the timer sounds, quick release the pressure. Transfer the meatballs to a serving platter and garnish with the remaining crushed pineapple.

10. Whisk the cornstarch slurry, add it to the pot, select Sauté, and cook, stirring, for about 5 minutes until the sauce is bubbly and thickens. Drizzle some of the sauce on the meatballs and serve the remaining sauce on the side.

VARIATION: Substitute other ground meats (beef, pork, turkey) for the chicken. If avoiding soy, substitute coconut aminos or a bottled or homemade soy-free soy sauce for the soy sauce.

CHICKEN AND VEGETABLE LETTUCE CUPS

Whenever I think about lettuce cups, I think about my aunts making this dish for Chinese New Year and other big family celebrations. When my children were little, they loved filling their lettuce cups with the meat mixture and drizzling them with sauce. Lettuce cups became a tasty and fun way to eat their veggies. Iceberg lettuce is more common for the cups but requires more prep to trim it into shape. Butter lettuce is easier to use and serve because of the leaf shape.

SERVES 4

PREP TIME:
15 minutes

SAUTÉ:
12 minutes

PRESSURE BUILD:
5 minutes

PRESSURE COOK:
1 minute, high

PRESSURE RELEASE:
Quick

TOTAL TIME:
33 minutes

3 teaspoons cornstarch, divided

1 tablespoon water, plus ¼ cup, divided

1 pound ground chicken

1 tablespoon oyster sauce

1 tablespoon light soy sauce

1 teaspoon neutral oil

1 medium sweet onion, chopped

2 garlic cloves, minced

2 carrots, chopped

1 (8-ounce) can water chestnuts, drained and diced

2 scallions, white and green parts, chopped

1 tablespoon hoisin sauce, plus ¼ cup, divided

1 head butter lettuce, leaves separated

1. In a small bowl, whisk 2 teaspoons of cornstarch and 1 tablespoon of water to make the slurry. Set aside.

2. In a medium bowl, mix the chicken, oyster sauce, soy sauce, and remaining 1 teaspoon of cornstarch. Set aside.

3. On the Instant Pot, select Sauté and adjust the heat to high. While the pot preheats, pour in the oil and add the onion. Stir-fry for about 3 minutes until slightly browned.

4. Add the chicken and garlic, spreading it out. Brown for 1 minute, then stir-fry for about 3 minutes until no longer pink.

5. Add the carrots and remaining ¼ cup of water to deglaze the pot, scraping up any browned bits from the bottom.

6. Lock the lid. Program to pressure cook for 1 minute on high pressure.

7. When the timer sounds, quick release the pressure. Carefully remove the lid.

8. Select Sauté, whisk the cornstarch slurry, and stir it into the pot. Add the water chestnuts, scallions, and 1 tablespoon of hoisin sauce. Cook for about 2 minutes, stirring, until the sauce thickens slightly.

9. Transfer the filling to a serving bowl and serve with lettuce cups and the remaining ¼ cup of hoisin sauce on the side.

INGREDIENT TIP: Use peeled, diced jicama as a water chestnut substitute (add it to the pot in step 5) and/or plum sauce if you don't have hoisin sauce.

HONEY AND SOY SAUCE CHICKEN WINGS

This recipe is easy to make with very little hands-on time. You can prepare it ahead by marinating the chicken wings overnight and then cooking them in the Instant Pot about 20 minutes before you want to eat. There's room in the Instant Pot if you want to double the recipe for a large group.

SERVES 6

PREP TIME:
10 minutes,
plus
30 minutes
to marinate

**PRESSURE
BUILD:**
10 minutes

**PRESSURE
COOK:**
5 minutes,
high

**PRESSURE
RELEASE:**
Natural,
5 minutes

TOTAL TIME:
1 hour

2½ pounds chicken wing pieces
2 tablespoons light soy sauce
2 tablespoons honey
1 tablespoon hoisin sauce
1 teaspoon sesame oil

1 teaspoon garlic powder
1 teaspoon chili oil (optional)
½ teaspoon salt
½ cup water

1. In a large zip-top bag, combine the chicken wings, soy sauce, honey, hoisin sauce, sesame oil, garlic powder, chili oil (if using), and salt. Seal the bag and shake to coat. Refrigerate to marinate for 30 minutes, or overnight.

2. Place the wings, marinade, and water in the Instant Pot.

3. Lock the lid. Program to pressure cook in Poultry mode for 5 minutes on high pressure.

4. When the timer sounds, let the pressure release naturally for 5 minutes, then quick release the remaining pressure. Carefully remove the lid.

5. The wings are ready to eat, but if you want crispy skin, broil the wings in a preheated oven or in a preheated air-fryer for 1 to 2 minutes. Check frequently, so they do not burn.

VARIATION: You can use other chicken parts for this recipe, but you'll need to adjust the cook time accordingly. Chicken drumsticks are ready in about 7 minutes. Chicken breasts are ready in 8 to 10 minutes, depending on their thickness.

STEAMED BEEF MEATBALLS

Some Chinese restaurants serve tea and dim sum for brunch or lunch. Dim sum dishes are small plates of steamed dumplings and other small bites you can order from a menu or from a server pushing a cart or carrying a tray. A party of four typically orders 10 to 12 different small plates. It's a labor-intensive effort to make 10 to 12 different dim sum dishes for one meal, but making a family-size recipe of steamed beef meatballs, a dim sum favorite, might satisfy those dim sum cravings.

**MAKES
8 MEATBALLS**

PREP TIME:
20 minutes,
plus
10 minutes
to marinate

**PRESSURE
BUILD:**
5 minutes

**PRESSURE
COOK:**
7 minutes,
high

**PRESSURE
RELEASE:**
Natural,
5 minutes

TOTAL TIME:
47 minutes

1 pound lean ground beef
½ cup chopped fresh cilantro leaves
4 tablespoons cold water, divided,
  plus 1 cup
4 teaspoons light soy sauce
1 tablespoon cornstarch
1 teaspoon sugar

¼ teaspoon salt
⅛ teaspoon baking soda
⅛ teaspoon ground white pepper
1 large iceberg lettuce or
  cabbage leaf
1 to 2 teaspoons
  Worcestershire sauce

1. In a medium bowl, combine the ground beef, cilantro, 2 tablespoons of water, soy sauce, cornstarch, sugar, salt, baking soda, and pepper. Use a wooden spoon or chopsticks to mix the ingredients, then stir in one direction for about 5 minutes until the meat becomes paste-like, adding up to 1 tablespoon more of water, if needed. Set aside to marinate for 10 minutes.

2. Pour 1 cup of water (it does not need to be cold) into the Instant Pot and place a trivet inside. Line a pressure-safe bowl with the lettuce leaf and pour in the remaining 1 tablespoon of water.

3. Divide the meat into 8 equal portions and roll each into a meatball. Place the meatballs on the lettuce leaf and place the bowl on the trivet.

4. Lock the lid. Program to pressure cook for 7 minutes on high pressure.

5. When the timer sounds, let the pressure release naturally for 5 minutes, then quick release the remaining pressure.

6. Sprinkle with Worcestershire sauce to taste and serve.

SHRIMP RICE PAPER ROLLS

These shrimp rice paper rolls are an easy hack of one of my favorite dim sum dishes, shrimp rice noodle rolls. Buy fresh shrimp only if you know it's very fresh and you can use it on the same day. Frozen shrimp is convenient and thaws quickly. If allergic to shrimp, substitute char siu (barbecue pork) or stir-fried Chinese chives or mushrooms.

SERVES 4

PREP TIME:
35 minutes

PRESSURE BUILD:
10 minutes

PRESSURE COOK:
4 minutes, high

PRESSURE RELEASE:
Quick

TOTAL TIME:
49 minutes

4 round rice paper sheets

Lettuce or cabbage leaves, for lining bowls

4 tablespoons water, divided, plus 1½ cups

8 ounces jumbo (26 count) shrimp, peeled and deveined

2 tablespoons light soy sauce

1 teaspoon sugar

½ teaspoon chicken bouillon

1 tablespoon fried shallot or onion (optional)

1 tablespoon chopped scallion, white and green parts (optional)

1. Fill a large bowl with water. One at a time, drop the rice paper sheets into the water and soak for 5 minutes. Set aside while preparing the remaining ingredients.

2. Line two pressure-safe bowls with lettuce leaves and add 1 tablespoon of water to each bowl. Set aside.

3. Place a sheet of rice paper on a work surface and arrange 3 shrimp on the bottom third of the sheet. Roll up the sheet halfway, tuck in the sides, and roll it the rest of the way. Place the roll in a prepared bowl and repeat to make one more shrimp roll.

4. Pour 1 cup of water into the Instant Pot and place a trivet inside. Place the filled bowl on the trivet.

5. Lock the lid. Program to pressure cook for 2 minutes on high pressure.

6. While the first two rolls steam, roll the remaining shrimp and rice sheets (repeat step 3) and place them in the second prepared bowl.

7. When the timer sounds, quick release the pressure and carefully remove the lid and bowl.

8. Pour the remaining ½ cup of water into the pot and repeat the process (steps 4 and 5) for steaming the second batch.

9. In a small bowl, stir together the soy sauce, remaining 2 tablespoons of water, sugar, and chicken bouillon. Drizzle each steamed roll with 1 teaspoon of sauce and garnish with fried shallot (if using) and scallion (if using). Cut the rolls into thirds and serve with any extra sauce on the side.

INGREDIENT TIP: You can find round rice paper sheets at well-stocked supermarkets. Use leftover rice paper sheets to make plain rice rolls or fill them with 2 tablespoons cooked meat and stir-fried vegetables. Rice paper will feel pliable quickly, but soaking it for 5 minutes softens the paper so it's tender when cooked. The rice paper will stick and tear while cooking without a layer of lettuce or cabbage lining the bowl.

WONTONS WITH CHICKEN AND PORK STOCK

Wontons floating in a bowl of chicken and pork stock with fresh chopped scallion and a pinch of white pepper are heavenly. You can make this dish into a full meal by adding cooked Chinese vegetables, noodles, barbecue pork, Chinese-style roast duck, or a ladle of beef stew. Be sure to pinch the edges of the wonton skin together and err on the side of making small wontons rather than overfilling them so they don't burst.

SERVES 4

PREP TIME:
1 hour

SAUTÉ:
15 minutes

TOTAL TIME:
1 hour
15 minutes

8 ounces shrimp, peeled and deveined

2 teaspoons finely grated fresh ginger

8 ounces ground pork

1 cup chopped scallion, white and green parts, plus more for garnish

1 tablespoon oyster sauce

1 tablespoon light soy sauce

2 teaspoons cornstarch

2 teaspoons sesame oil

Ground white pepper

40 wonton skins

8 cups Chicken and Pork Stock (page 33)

1. Chop the shrimp into the size of peas and place them in a medium bowl.

2. Add the ginger ground pork, scallion, oyster sauce, soy sauce, cornstarch, sesame oil, and ¼ teaspoon of pepper and mix well.

3. Line a rimmed baking sheet with parchment paper.

4. Open the package of wonton skins by cutting off one edge. Keep the skins in the package to avoid drying them out. Place a small bowl of water nearby.

5. Place a wonton skin on a clean, dry, flat surface with a bottom corner closest to you. Use a spoon to scoop a grape-size amount of filling and place it in the center of the wonton skin. Dip your finger into the water, wet the edges of the wonton skin, and fold up the bottom corner so it forms a triangle. Pinch the edges together firmly but without tearing the skin. Wet the three points of the triangle and bring the left and right points up to the center, folding the top point down. (Your wonton should look like a stuffed envelope.) Place it on the prepared baking sheet and repeat until all the filling is used (space the wontons apart so they don't touch).

6. Pour the stock into the Instant Pot, select Sauté, and bring to a boil.

7. Add the wontons and gently stir so they don't stick to the bottom of the pot. Cook until the wontons float, then continue to boil for 3 to 4 minutes until cooked through and the shrimp are pink. If you can't see the shrimp through the wrapper, cut one in half to check for doneness.

8. Serve the wontons in the stock with a sprinkle of scallion and a light sprinkle of pepper.

VARIATION: For a shellfish-free option, omit the shrimp and use 1 pound ground pork instead. Swap the oyster sauce for ½ teaspoon salt and 1 teaspoon sugar. You can add umami by adding a handful of rehydrated and minced shiitake mushrooms.

SERVING TIP: Add a drizzle of chili oil to the wontons for some heat.

LION HEAD MEATBALL SOUP

(PORK, NAPA CABBAGE, AND VERMICELLI SOUP)

This recipe is inspired by a traditional Chinese dish called lion head meatball, a softball-size pork meatball that is fried, steamed, and served family-style. Smaller meatballs are easier to cook and serve, however, and take less time.

SERVES 6

PREP TIME:
30 minutes

PRESSURE BUILD:
10 minutes

PRESSURE COOK:
5 minutes, high

PRESSURE RELEASE:
Natural, 5 minutes

TOTAL TIME:
50 minutes

3 ounces (2 bundles) mung bean vermicelli

4 scallions, white and green parts, thinly sliced, divided

1 pound ground pork

1 cup panko or regular bread crumbs

2 large eggs, lightly beaten

2 tablespoons light soy sauce

1 tablespoon cornstarch

2 teaspoons grated fresh ginger, or 1 teaspoon ground ginger

¼ teaspoon salt

Ground white pepper

1½ pounds (1 small head) napa cabbage, chopped into bite-size pieces

4 cups Chicken Stock with Ginger (page 32) or store-bought chicken broth

1. In a large bowl, soak the vermicelli in water for about 15 minutes until soft. Measure ¼ cup of sliced scallion and set aside.

2. In a medium bowl, combine the ground pork, bread crumbs, eggs, remaining scallions, soy sauce, cornstarch, ginger, salt, and ½ teaspoon of pepper. Stir in one direction for about 5 minutes until the meat forms a paste. Set aside.

3. Place the cabbage in the Instant Pot. Drain the vermicelli and place it on the cabbage. Pour in the stock.

4. Divide the meat mixture into 8 equal portions and form each into a meatball. Arrange the meatballs on the vermicelli.

5. Lock the lid. Program to pressure cook for 5 minutes on high pressure. When the timer sounds, release the pressure naturally for 5 minutes, then quick release the remaining pressure.

6. Place the cabbage, vermicelli, and broth in a large serving bowl and top with the meatballs. Garnish with the reserved scallions and season with pepper.

FIVE-SPICE BEEF SHANK

Chinese banquets often include a cold appetizer platter as a first course, and five-spice beef shank is usually one of them. The braised beef shanks are cooked, then marinated overnight in the refrigerator, which also makes them easier to slice thinly before serving. There's room in the Instant Pot to make two same-size beef shanks without needing to double the sauce ingredients.

SERVES 6

PREP TIME:
20 minutes,
plus
overnight
to chill and
marinate

SAUTÉ:
5 minutes

**PRESSURE
BUILD:**
10 minutes

**PRESSURE
COOK:**
15 minutes,
high

**PRESSURE
RELEASE:**
Natural,
30 minutes

TOTAL TIME:
1 hour
20 minutes,
plus
overnight

1 (1½-pound) beef shank
8 cups water
4 cups beef broth or water
¼ cup light soy sauce
2 tablespoons dark soy sauce
2 tablespoons brown sugar

1 teaspoon Chinese
five-spice powder
1 teaspoon dried Valencia orange
peel (optional)
2 star anise pods (optional)

1. Place the beef shank in the Instant Pot and pour in the water. Select Sauté and bring the water to a boil. Parboil for 5 minutes, or until the water starts to foam. Select Cancel.

2. Rinse the shank to remove any impurities. Rinse and dry the liner before returning it to the base.

3. Return the shank to the Instant Pot, then add the broth, light and dark soy sauces, brown sugar, five-spice powder, orange peel (if using), and star anise (if using).

4. Lock the lid. Program to pressure cook for 15 minutes on high pressure

5. When the timer sounds, let the pressure release naturally for about 30 minutes.

6. Transfer the beef and sauce to a large heatproof container and let cool to room temperature. Refrigerate, covered, overnight.

7. Thinly slice the beef and serve warm or at room temperature.

INGREDIENT TIP: Beef shank can also be called banana beef shank or beef D shank and varies in size. The smaller shanks taste better and cook more evenly. Beef shanks that weigh 2 pounds or more need to cook for 20 minutes. Strain and reserve the cooking liquid as a master sauce (see page 6).

STOCKS AND SOUPS

Bok Choy, Pork, and Vermicelli Soup, page 34

CHICKEN STOCK WITH GINGER

This chicken stock with ginger is clear and savory, with a sweet spiciness. Ginger aids digestion and has antiviral and anti-inflammatory health benefits. If your stock becomes gelatinous when refrigerated, it's because the stock is protein- and collagen-rich. Use a cut-up whole chicken or a combination of chicken breasts and chicken stock parts (neck, back, ribs, etc.).

MAKES 12 CUPS

PREP TIME:
10 minutes

SAUTÉ:
5 minutes

PRESSURE BUILD:
20 minutes

PRESSURE COOK:
60 minutes, high

PRESSURE RELEASE:
Natural, 30 minutes

TOTAL TIME:
2 hours 15 minutes

5 pounds chicken parts
16 cups water, divided, plus more as needed

1 (2-inch) piece fresh ginger, thinly sliced
1 teaspoon salt

1. Place the chicken in the Instant Pot and pour in 4 cups of water. Select Sauté and bring the water to a boil. Parboil for 5 minutes, or until the water starts to foam. Select Cancel.

2. In a large colander in the sink, drain the chicken and rinse it to remove any impurities. Rinse and dry the liner before returning it to the base.

3. Return the chicken to the Instant Pot and pour in the remaining 12 cups of water, or as needed to reach the maximum fill line. Add the ginger and salt.

4. Lock the lid. Program to pressure cook using the Soup function for 60 minutes on high pressure.

5. When the timer sounds, let the pressure release naturally for 30 minutes, then quick release any remaining pressure.

6. Carefully remove the lid. Remove the chicken (reserve the meat for other uses) and strain the stock through a fine-mesh sieve into a large pot. Or, if using the stock later, transfer to Mason jars or freezer-safe containers and cool in an ice bath. Refrigerate for up to 1 week, or freeze for up to 2 months.

CHICKEN AND PORK STOCK

This chicken and pork stock is a savory base for making soups such as Wontons with Chicken and Pork Stock (page 33) and other noodle soups. Select lean pork, such as pork tenderloin or pork sirloin. Buy a bone-in pork shoulder or pork blade roast, trim off the fat, and use the bones and some of the meat for stock. Look for soup bones that are mostly from the femur, with knuckles and marrow.

MAKES 12 CUPS

PREP TIME:
15 minutes

SAUTE:
10 minutes

PRESSURE BUILD:
30 minutes

PRESSURE COOK:
60 minutes, high

PRESSURE RELEASE:
Natural, 30 minutes

TOTAL TIME:
2 hours 25 minutes

2 pounds bone-in skin-on chicken breasts or drumsticks
1 pound lean pork, cut into 4 pieces
1 pound pork bones
16 cups water, divided, plus more as needed
1 (1-inch) piece fresh ginger, thinly sliced
2 teaspoons salt

1. In the Instant Pot, combine the chicken, pork, and pork bones, then pour in 4 cups of water. Select Sauté and bring to a boil. Parboil for 10 minutes, or until foam starts to form. Select Cancel.

2. In a large colander in the sink, drain the chicken, pork, and bones and rinse them to remove any impurities. Rinse and dry the pot before returning it to the base.

3. Return the chicken, pork, and pork bones to the Instant Pot and add the ginger and salt. Pour in the remaining 12 cups of water, or as needed to reach the maximum fill line.

4. Lock the lid. Program to pressure cook using the Soup function for 60 minutes on high pressure.

5. When the timer sounds, let the pressure release naturally for 30 minutes, then quick release any remaining pressure.

6. Carefully remove the lid. Remove the chicken, pork, and bones (reserve the meat for other uses) and strain the stock through a fine-mesh sieve into a large pot. Or, if using the stock later, transfer to Mason jars or freezer-safe containers and cool in an ice bath. Refrigerate for up to 1 week, or freeze for up to 2 months.

BOK CHOY, PORK, AND VERMICELLI SOUP

My mom buys dried bok choy from Chinatown to make a soup to soothe scratchy throats and coughs. My version is made using fresh bok choy, which has a milder flavor. Mung bean vermicelli noodles are dried bundles of noodles. To halve the noodle bundles, cut at the folded end.

SERVES 6

PREP TIME:
20 minutes

SAUTÉ:
7 minutes

PRESSURE BUILD:
7 minutes

PRESSURE COOK:
1 minute, high

PRESSURE RELEASE:
Natural, 5 minutes

TOTAL TIME:
40 minutes

1 bundle mung bean rice vermicelli

8 ounces baby bok choy

4 ounces lean pork, thinly sliced or julienned

1 teaspoon rice wine

¼ teaspoon salt

Ground white pepper

1 teaspoon cornstarch

1 teaspoon neutral oil

1 (½-inch) piece fresh ginger, thinly sliced

4 cups Chicken Stock with Ginger (page 32) or Chicken and Pork Stock (page 33)

2 carrots, cut into ¼-inch rounds

2 tablespoons chopped scallion, white and green parts

1. In a medium bowl, soak the mung bean vermicelli in cold water for 5 minutes. Drain and use scissors to cut the vermicelli in half. Set aside.

2. If the baby bok choy are 2 to 3 inches long, halve them lengthwise; otherwise chop them crosswise into 1-inch pieces. Set aside.

3. In a small bowl, mix the pork, wine, salt, and ¼ teaspoon of pepper. Add the cornstarch and mix again. Set aside.

4. On the Instant Pot, select Sauté to preheat the pot. Once hot, pour in the oil and add the ginger. Stir-fry for 1 minute until fragrant. Add the pork mixture and stir-fry for about 2 minutes until no longer pink.

5. Pour in the stock to deglaze the pot, scraping up any browned bits from the bottom. Add the carrots, bok choy, and vermicelli.

6. Lock the lid. Program to pressure cook for 1 minute on high pressure.

7. When the timer sounds, let the pressure release naturally for 5 minutes, then quick release the remaining pressure.

8. Serve with a sprinkle of scallion and a pinch of pepper.

VARIATION: Make this vegan by substituting 8 ounces fresh mushrooms, sliced, for the pork and using store-bought vegetable broth instead of chicken stock.

CHICKEN AND SWEET CORN SOUP

If you love creamed corn, you will love this soup. It is a comforting chicken soup to have when it's cold outside. Layer the drumsticks on top so it's easy to remove the chicken bones before serving. Alternatively, use boneless, skinless chicken thighs or breasts.

SERVES 6

PREP TIME:
10 minutes

SAUTÉ:
5 minutes

PRESSURE BUILD:
20 minutes

PRESSURE COOK:
11 minutes, high

PRESSURE RELEASE:
Natural, 15 minutes

TOTAL TIME:
1 hour 1 minute

3 tablespoons cornstarch

3 tablespoons water

2 (15-ounce) cans creamed corn

4 cups Chicken Stock with Ginger (page 32)

1 cup frozen corn kernels

1 tablespoon rice wine

2 garlic cloves, minced

1 (½-inch) piece fresh ginger, minced

½ teaspoon salt

¼ teaspoon ground white pepper

1½ pounds chicken drumsticks, skin removed

2 large eggs, lightly beaten

¼ cup chopped scallion, white and green parts (optional)

1. In a small bowl, whisk the cornstarch and water. Set aside.

2. In the Instant Pot, combine the creamed corn, stock, corn kernels, wine, garlic, ginger, salt, and pepper. Place the drumsticks on top.

3. Lock the lid. Program to pressure cook using the Soup function for 11 minutes on high pressure.

4. When the timer sounds, let the pressure release naturally for 15 minutes, then quick release any remaining pressure.

5. Carefully remove the lid and select Sauté. Transfer the drumsticks to a bowl, remove and discard the bones, shred the meat, and return the meat to the pot.

6. Whisk the cornstarch slurry, pour it into the pot, and stir the soup. Slowly drizzle in the eggs in a circular motion, then stir the soup gently. Ladle it into bowls and garnish each with a sprinkle of scallion (if using).

VARIATION: Make it vegan by substituting vegetable broth for chicken stock and replacing the drumsticks with tofu cubes. Add the tofu with the cornstarch slurry. Swap the eggs for vegan eggs.

LUO SONG TANG (BEEF AND VEGETABLE SOUP)

This beef and vegetable soup is known as *luo song tang*, which means borscht soup. Russian chefs living and working in Shanghai modified their traditional borscht using tomatoes instead of beets. This soup is typically served in Chinese restaurants featuring Hong Kong–style Western cuisine.

SERVES 6

PREP TIME:
20 minutes

SAUTÉ:
15 minutes

PRESSURE BUILD:
15 minutes

PRESSURE COOK:
30 minutes, high

PRESSURE RELEASE:
Natural, 20 minutes

TOTAL TIME:
1 hour 40 minutes

1 pound beef stew meat

½ teaspoon salt

½ teaspoon freshly ground black pepper or ground white pepper

3 teaspoons neutral oil, divided

1 sweet onion, chopped

2 garlic cloves, chopped

4 cups beef broth or broth of choice

1½ cups chopped carrot (from about 3 carrots)

1½ cups chopped celery (from about 4 stalks)

1½ cups chopped peeled potato (from about 3 potatoes)

1½ cups chopped tomato (from about 3 tomatoes)

3 tablespoons tomato paste

4 cups chopped red or green cabbage (about ½ head)

1. Pat the beef dry with paper towels and sprinkle the beef with the salt and pepper.

2. On the Instant Pot, select Sauté and adjust the heat to high to preheat the pot. Once it's hot, pour in 2 teaspoons of oil and add the beef. Brown the beef on all sides for about 5 minutes. Transfer the meat to a plate.

3. Pour the remaining 1 teaspoon of oil into the pot and add the onion and garlic. Stir-fry for about 3 minutes until the onion browns slightly and the garlic is fragrant. Add the broth to deglaze the pot, scraping up any browned bits from the bottom.

4. Return the beef to the pot and add the carrot, celery, potato, tomato, and tomato paste. Stir to combine. Add the cabbage.

5. Lock the lid. Program to pressure cook using the Soup function for 30 minutes on high pressure.

6. When the timer sounds, release the pressure naturally for 20 minutes, then quick release the remaining pressure. Carefully remove the lid and serve.

WESTLAKE SOUP (MINCED BEEF AND EGG SOUP)

Westlake soup is a light soup with a thick broth. Use any cut of beef, though thinly sliced beef cut for stir-fry will reduce the amount of mincing time required. You can also use other proteins here, such as minced chicken, minced lean pork, or thinly sliced white fish fillets, like cod or sole.

SERVES 4

PREP TIME:
20 minutes

SAUTÉ:
5 minutes

PRESSURE BUILD:
15 minutes

PRESSURE COOK:
5 minutes, high

PRESSURE RELEASE:
Natural, 10 minutes

TOTAL TIME:
55 minutes

4 ounces beef

1 teaspoon light soy sauce

1 teaspoon neutral oil

4 ounces mushrooms (any kind), chopped

6 ounces silken or soft tofu, drained and cut into ½-inch cubes

¼ teaspoon salt

Ground white pepper

4 cups Chicken Stock with Ginger (page 32)

3 tablespoons water

3 tablespoons cornstarch

4 large egg whites, lightly beaten, or 2 large eggs

1 cup chopped fresh cilantro, plus more for serving

1. To mince the beef, using a cleaver or large chef's knife, cut the beef into strips and then into small cubes before chopping until the beef is minced. Transfer to a small bowl and stir in the soy sauce. Set aside.

2. On the Instant Pot, select Sauté to preheat the pot. Once hot, pour in the oil and add the mushrooms. Stir-fry for 3 to 4 minutes until the mushrooms are soft.

3. Add the beef, tofu, salt, and ⅛ teaspoon of pepper and pour in the stock.

4. Lock the lid. Program to pressure cook using the Soup function for 5 minutes on high pressure.

5. In a small bowl, whisk the water and cornstarch. Set aside.

6. When the timer sounds, let the pressure release naturally for 10 minutes, then quick release the remaining pressure. Carefully remove the lid.

7. Select Sauté. Whisk the cornstarch slurry, then stir it into the soup. Cook for about 2 minutes, or until the soup begins to bubble and thicken.

8. Slowly drizzle in the egg whites. Wait 15 seconds, then stir gently in one direction. Add the cilantro.

9. Serve the soup with a pinch of pepper and more cilantro, as desired.

VARIATION: Make the recipe vegetarian by omitting the beef, using more mushrooms, adding a chopped onion in step 3, and using vegetable broth instead of chicken stock.

HOT AND SOUR TOFU AND VEGETABLE SOUP

Hot and sour soup is a Chinese soup that is pure comfort and will warm you on a cold day. I like to add lots of bamboo and mushrooms, so the soup is more filling and heartier.

SERVES 4

PREP TIME:
15 minutes

SAUTÉ:
15 minutes

PRESSURE BUILD:
10 minutes

PRESSURE COOK:
1 minute, high

PRESSURE RELEASE:
Quick

TOTAL TIME:
41 minutes

3 tablespoons cornstarch

2 tablespoons rice vinegar or black vinegar

1 tablespoon light soy sauce

1 teaspoon neutral oil

8 ounces mushrooms (any type), chopped

¼ teaspoon salt

4 cups vegetable broth

14 ounces soft or silken tofu, cut into ½-inch cubes

2 large carrots, julienned (about 1 cup)

½ (8-ounce) can bamboo shoots, julienned

Ground white pepper or freshly ground black pepper

2 large eggs, lightly beaten

1 teaspoon chili oil (optional)

¼ cup chopped scallion, white and green parts, or fresh cilantro

1. In a small bowl, whisk the cornstarch, vinegar, and soy sauce. Set aside.

2. On the Instant Pot, select Sauté to preheat the pot. Once hot, pour in the oil and add the mushrooms and salt. Stir-fry for about 2 minutes until soft.

3. Pour in the broth and add the tofu, carrots, bamboo shoots, and ½ teaspoon of pepper.

4. Lock the lid. Program to pressure cook using the Soup function for 1 minute on high pressure.

5. When the timer sounds, quick release the pressure. Carefully remove the lid.

6. Select Sauté. Whisk the cornstarch slurry, then stir it into the soup. Cook until the soup bubbles, then drizzle in the eggs in a circular motion. Wait 15 seconds, add the chili oil (if using; alternatively add chili oil to taste in each bowl after serving), then stir the soup gently. Select Cancel.

7. Serve garnished with a sprinkle of chopped scallion and a light sprinkle of pepper.

VARIATION: Make this soup more savory by adding 4 ounces julienned chicken or pork in step 2. To make it more traditional, add sliced shiitake mushrooms or wood ear mushrooms in step 3.

SCALLOP, SHRIMP, AND CRAB SOUP

Make this seafood soup anytime with ingredients in your freezer and pantry. Buy frozen bay scallops and frozen bay shrimp for consistent quality and ease of use—they thaw in minutes. Canned crabmeat is convenient and ready to use and adds to the body of the broth.

SERVES 6

PREP TIME:
20 minutes

SAUTÉ:
5 minutes

PRESSURE BUILD:
15 minutes

PRESSURE COOK:
2 minutes, high

PRESSURE RELEASE:
Natural, 5 minutes

TOTAL TIME:
47 minutes

6 ounces frozen bay scallops, thawed

6 ounces frozen bay shrimp, thawed

3 carrots, chopped

1½ cups frozen corn kernels

8 ounces soft or silken tofu, diced small

2 garlic cloves, minced

½ teaspoon salt

¼ teaspoon ground white pepper

4 cups water, plus 3 tablespoons, divided

3 tablespoons cornstarch

1 (6-ounce) can crabmeat, drained

6 ounces snow peas or snap peas, halved, fibrous end and string removed

2 large eggs, lightly beaten

2 scallions, white and green parts, chopped

1. In a medium bowl, combine the scallops with enough water to cover and swish to release any sand. Repeat, changing the water as needed, until the scallops are clean and free of sand. Set aside. Peel the shrimp, if needed.

2. In the Instant Pot, combine the carrots, corn kernels, tofu, and garlic. Add the scallops, shrimp, salt, ¼ teaspoon of pepper, and 4 cups of water.

3. Lock the lid. Program to pressure cook using the Soup function for 2 minutes on high pressure.

4. In a small bowl, whisk the cornstarch and remaining 3 tablespoons of water. Set aside.

5. When the timer sounds, let the pressure release naturally for 5 minutes, then quick release the remaining pressure. Carefully remove the lid.

6. Select Sauté and add the crabmeat and snow peas. Whisk the cornstarch slurry, then add it to the soup and stir to combine. Cook for about 4 minutes until the soup begins to bubble and thicken.

7. Slowly drizzle in the eggs in a circular motion. Wait 15 seconds, then stir gently.

8. Serve with a pinch of pepper and chopped scallions as garnish.

VARIATION: Use any colorful but sturdy vegetables you want in this soup (4 cups total), such as asparagus, mushrooms, peas, or red bell peppers. Use any shrimp shells that you save (for example, from Shrimp and Asparagus Stir-Fry, page 86) to give this soup extra flavor by pressure cooking the shells in 4 cups of water for 5 minutes and then straining and discarding the shells. Use the flavorful liquid for step 2. Allow an extra 15 minutes for this step.

MOM'S BEEF MEATBALL, POTATO, AND CARROT SOUP

My mom would make this comforting soup for me whenever I felt sick. It's easier to mince beef with a cleaver than with a chef's knife. If you prefer to use ground beef, select extra-lean ground beef. Ginger and garlic have antiviral health benefits and ginger is great for digestion.

SERVES 6

PREP TIME:
25 minutes

PRESSURE BUILD:
15 minutes

PRESSURE COOK:
5 minutes, high

PRESSURE RELEASE:
Natural, 10 minutes

TOTAL TIME:
55 minutes

8 ounces lean beef (any tender cut) or lean ground beef

1 teaspoon cornstarch

Ground white pepper

4 cups Chicken Stock with Ginger (page 32) or water

4 carrots, chopped (about 1½ cups)

2 large potatoes, peeled and chopped (about 1½ cups)

1 (½-inch) piece fresh ginger, minced

1 garlic clove, chopped

½ teaspoon salt

¼ cup chopped scallion, white and green parts

1. If mincing the beef, using a cleaver or a large chef's knife, cut the beef into strips, then into small cubes, and then mince it. Transfer the beef to a medium bowl and stir in the cornstarch and ⅛ teaspoon of pepper. Divide the meat mixture into 8 equal portions and shape each into a meatball.

2. In the Instant Pot, combine the stock, carrots, potatoes, ginger, garlic, and salt. Place the meatballs on top.

3. Lock the lid. Program to pressure cook using the Soup function for 5 minutes on high pressure.

4. When the timer sounds, let the pressure release naturally for 10 minutes, then quick release the remaining pressure.

5. Serve with a sprinkle of chopped scallion and a pinch of pepper.

VARIATION: Instead of beef, use sliced fish fillets or other ground meats, such as chicken, lean pork, or turkey. For a faster meal, buy prepared meatballs from an Asian market.

RED BEAN AND TAPIOCA TONG SUI

One of the best Cantonese traditions is ending a meal with a bowl of *tong sui*, a dessert soup, which literally means "sugar water." One of my favorite varieties is a red bean soup with small tapioca pearls. The small, round red beans are also known as adzuki beans. Dried Valencia orange peel (or more traditionally, dried mandarin peel) adds a bright citrus flavor to the soup.

SERVES 6

PREP TIME:
5 minutes

SAUTÉ:
20 minutes

PRESSURE BUILD:
15 minutes

PRESSURE COOK:
45 minutes, high

PRESSURE RELEASE:
Natural, 15 minutes

TOTAL TIME:
1 hour 40 minutes

6 cups water

1 cup dried adzuki beans, rinsed and picked over for debris

1 teaspoon dried Valencia orange peel

½ cup (3 to 4 ounces) rock sugar

⅓ cup small tapioca pearls

1. Pour the water into the Instant Pot and add the beans and Valencia peel.

2. Lock the lid. Program to pressure cook for 45 minutes on high pressure.

3. When the timer sounds, let the pressure release naturally for 15 minutes.

4. Carefully remove the lid. Select Sauté and adjust the heat to low. Add the rock sugar and tapioca pearls. Cook for about 20 minutes, stirring every 5 minutes, or until the tapioca pearls are translucent and no longer white.

5. Select Cancel, then select Keep Warm until ready to serve.

INGREDIENT TIP: If you don't have rock sugar, use ⅓ cup granulated sugar. Rock sugar looks like golden rocks because it is crystalized sugar syrup. It is irregular in size and difficult to measure; I used 3 Ping-Pong ball–size lumps to sweeten the soup lightly. You can also use rock sugar in any recipe that uses the red braise method (see page 66) to give the meat a glossy, shiny appearance. If you have aged and dried mandarin peels, use one piece for its medicinal properties.

BEEF, LAMB, AND PORK

Lu Rao Fan (Braised Pork and Egg Rice Bowl),
page 68

BLACK PEPPER FLANK STEAK

Flank steak is an easy cut of beef to prepare, and it is tender when pressure cooked. Because there's minimal evaporation in the Instant Pot, this recipe makes a lot of delicious sauce to enjoy over rice or noodles.

SERVES 4

PREP TIME:
10 minutes, plus 10 minutes to marinate

SAUTÉ:
10 minutes

PRESSURE BUILD:
5 minutes

PRESSURE COOK:
5 minutes, high

PRESSURE RELEASE:
Quick

TOTAL TIME:
40 minutes

1 pound flank steak

4 teaspoons light soy sauce, divided

3 teaspoons cornstarch, divided

1 teaspoon sugar

1 tablespoon water

1 tablespoon oyster sauce

1 teaspoon freshly ground black pepper

2 teaspoons neutral oil, divided

2 red bell peppers, chopped

½ sweet onion, sliced

¼ cup beef broth or water

Cooked rice or noodles, for serving

1. Using a sharp chef's knife, cut the flank steak with the grain into 4 strips, then cut the strips into ¼-inch-thick bite-size pieces. Transfer to a medium bowl. Stir in 3 teaspoons of soy sauce, 1 teaspoon of cornstarch, and the sugar. Set aside to marinate for 10 minutes.

2. In a small bowl, whisk the water, oyster sauce, remaining 1 teaspoon of soy sauce, remaining 2 teaspoons of cornstarch, and pepper. Set aside.

3. On the Instant Pot, select Sauté and adjust the heat to high. Pour in 1 teaspoon of oil. Once hot, add the bell peppers and stir-fry for 2 minutes until crisp-tender. Transfer the bell peppers to another medium bowl.

4. Pour the remaining 1 teaspoon of oil into the pot and add the onion. Stir-fry for about 2 minutes until soft. Add the beef, spreading it out, and stir-fry for 1 minute until browned. Pour in the broth to deglaze the pot, scraping up any browned bits from the bottom.

5. Lock the lid. Program to pressure cook for 5 minutes on high pressure.

6. When the timer sounds, quick release the pressure.

7. Carefully remove the lid, select Sauté again, and add the bell peppers. Whisk the cornstarch slurry and stir it into the pot. Cook, stirring, for about 1 minute until the sauce bubbles and thickens. Serve immediately with rice or noodles.

VARIATION: You can make this recipe with chicken, pork, or tofu instead of beef. Prepare chicken or pork in the same marinade as the beef. If you want a vegetarian option, press a container of drained firm or extra-firm tofu between paper towels for at least 1 hour and then marinate as directed, but omit the oyster sauce from the slurry and use 1 teaspoon sugar instead. Pressure cook the tofu for 1 minute, chicken for 3 minutes, or pork for 5 minutes.

BEEF AND BROCCOLI

Flat iron steak is my favorite cut of beef for making a beef stir-fry in a wok because it is very tender. I adapted this recipe by using the 0 minutes pressure cook method to avoid overcooking the beef. Some Instant Pot models must cook for a minimum of 1 minute, in which case set the timer for 1 minute; when the Instant Pot reaches pressure, select Cancel and quick release the pressure.

SERVES 4

PREP TIME:
10 minutes, plus 10 minutes to marinate

SAUTÉ:
5 minutes

PRESSURE BUILD:
5 minutes

PRESSURE COOK:
0 minutes, high

PRESSURE RELEASE:
Quick

TOTAL TIME:
30 minutes

1 pound flat iron steak

1 tablespoon oyster sauce

2 teaspoons light soy sauce

2 teaspoons cornstarch, divided

1 teaspoon sugar

1 tablespoon water

1 teaspoon olive oil

2 garlic cloves, minced

½ cup beef broth or water

4 cups (10 ounces) fresh broccoli florets

Cooked rice or noodles, for serving (optional)

1. Using a sharp chef's knife, halve the flat iron steak along the grain, then cut the halves against the grain into ¼-inch-thick bite-size pieces. Transfer to a medium bowl. Stir in the oyster sauce, soy sauce, 1 teaspoon of cornstarch, and the sugar. Set aside to marinate for 10 minutes.

2. In a small bowl, whisk the water and remaining 1 teaspoon of cornstarch. Set aside.

3. On the Instant Pot, select Sauté and adjust the heat to high to preheat the pot. Once hot, pour in the oil and add the garlic. Stir-fry for about 30 seconds until fragrant.

4. Add the beef, spreading it out to sear, and stir-fry for 1 minute until browned.

5. Pour in the broth to deglaze the pot, scraping up any browned bits from the bottom. Stir in the broccoli.

6. Lock the lid. Program to pressure cook for 0 minutes on high pressure (or 1 minute and quick release as soon as the pressure cooker seals).

7. When the timer sounds, quick release the pressure.

8. Carefully remove the lid. Select Sauté again. Whisk the cornstarch slurry, then stir it into the pot. Cook for about 2 minutes, or until the sauce bubbles and thickens

9. Serve as is, or with rice or noodles.

MAPO DOUFU WITH GROUND BEEF

Mapo doufu means "pockmarked grandmother's tofu." The dish was invented by a woman from the Chengdu region, and the name of the dish refers to her elderly and smallpox-scarred appearance. It's a spicy tofu dish simmered with a sauce made of doubanjiang (a fermented broad bean paste with red pepper flakes), douchi (fermented black soybeans), and Sichuan peppercorns. The original recipe was made with ground beef, but it's fine to use ground pork, ground chicken, or plant-based ground meat substitutes instead.

SERVES 4

PREP TIME:
20 minutes

SAUTÉ:
5 minutes

PRESSURE BUILD:
5 minutes

PRESSURE COOK:
1 minute, high

PRESSURE RELEASE:
Quick

TOTAL TIME:
31 minutes

2 tablespoons water

2 teaspoons cornstarch

1 tablespoon neutral oil

2 teaspoons Sichuan peppercorns (optional)

2 garlic cloves, minced

1 (½-inch) piece fresh ginger, minced

1 tablespoon doubanjiang

1 tablespoon douchi, rinsed (optional)

8 ounces ground beef

½ cup beef broth or water

1 pound silken tofu, drained and cut into 16 pieces

½ cup sliced scallion, white and green parts, divided

1 teaspoon chili oil

Cooked rice or noodles, for serving (optional)

1. In a small bowl, whisk the water and cornstarch. Set aside.

2. On the Instant Pot, select Sauté to preheat the pot. Once hot, pour in the oil and add the peppercorns (if using). Stir-fry for 1 minute until fragrant. Discard the peppercorns.

3. Add the garlic, ginger, doubanjiang, and douchi (if using) and stir-fry for 1 minute until fragrant.

4. Add the ground beef and stir-fry for 1 minute until lightly browned.

5. Select Cancel. Pour in the broth to deglaze the pot, scraping up any browned bits from the bottom. Drain any excess liquid and add the tofu.

6. Lock the lid. Program to pressure cook for 1 minute on high pressure.

7. When the timer sounds, quick release the pressure. Carefully remove the lid. Whisk the cornstarch slurry and add it and ¼ cup of scallion to the pot. Stir.

8. Transfer the mapo doufu to a serving bowl and drizzle with chili oil and the remaining ¼ cup of scallion. Serve as is, or with rice or noodles.

INGREDIENT TIP: If you don't have whole Sichuan peppercorns, add a small amount of ground Sichuan peppercorns or some of the solids from a chili oil in step 3, and adjust to taste in step 8. If you want to substitute something else for the doubanjiang, use ½ teaspoon hoisin sauce and ½ teaspoon chili oil.

CURRY OXTAIL STEW

A Chinese-style curry is an easy one-pot meal packed with vegetables and a great alternative for those who are soy-free or follow a low-sodium diet. I love making oxtail in the Instant Pot because it's fast and the meat is fall-off-the-bone tender and juicy. Warm any leftover curry with some frozen peas, corn, or tofu for a lighter meal the next day.

SERVES 6

PREP TIME:
15 minutes

SAUTÉ:
20 minutes

PRESSURE BUILD:
20 minutes

PRESSURE COOK:
30 minutes, high

PRESSURE RELEASE:
Natural, 20 minutes

TOTAL TIME:
1 hour 45 minutes

4 pounds oxtail pieces
1 teaspoon salt
1 teaspoon freshly ground black pepper
2 teaspoons neutral oil, divided
4 garlic cloves, chopped
1 sweet onion, chopped
1 pound carrots, chopped
6 celery stalks, chopped

4 cups water, divided
3 large potatoes, peeled and chopped
¼ cup curry powder
2 tablespoons tomato paste
1 tablespoon ground turmeric
Cooked rice or noodles, for serving (optional)

1. Trim off any large areas of excess fat around the outside of the oxtail pieces. Pat dry with paper towel, sprinkle with salt and pepper, then pat the spices into the meat and set aside.

2. On the Instant Pot, select Sauté and adjust the heat to high to preheat the pot. Once hot, pour in 1 teaspoon of oil and add half the oxtail pieces, fatty-side down, spaced apart. Cook for 4 to 5 minutes until it's easy to turn the oxtails over. Sear for 5 minutes more until all sides are browned, then remove and repeat with the remaining oxtail pieces.

3. Pour in the remaining 1 teaspoon of oil and add the garlic and onion. Stir-fry for about 2 minutes until fragrant.

4. Add the carrots and celery and stir-fry for 2 minutes until softened.

5. Pour in 1 cup of water to deglaze the pot, scraping up any browned bits from the bottom.

6. Return the oxtail pieces to the pot, placing the large pieces at the bottom of the pot and the smaller pieces on top. Pour in the remaining 3 cups of water. Add the potatoes, curry powder, tomato paste, and turmeric.

7. Lock the lid. Program to pressure cook for 30 minutes on high pressure.

8. When the timer sounds, let the pressure release naturally for 20 minutes. Carefully remove the lid, and, if desired, use a gravy separator to remove some of the fat before stirring. Serve as is, or with rice or noodles.

INGREDIENT TIP: I sprinkle freshly ground black pepper on the oxtail as a light crust to prevent the oxtails from sticking to the pot during searing, but there's also a health benefit. Black pepper aids the absorption of curcumin, the compound associated with turmeric's superfood status. Ground turmeric root is a spice that gives curries their bright yellow color. If on a low-sodium diet, omit or use less salt. A sprinkle of scallions is also a nice topping option.

FIVE-SPICE BEEF AND VEGETABLE STEW

Beef brisket is a nice cut for this Chinese-style beef stew. If you can, find beef drop flank, which is the cut Chinese restaurants use. A third option is use beef chuck roast, which is leaner and will taste better cut into large pieces. Chop the vegetables into big pieces so they can cook together with the beef and, mostly, stay intact. Serve with cooked rice or quinoa.

SERVES 6

PREP TIME:
20 minutes

SAUTÉ:
10 minutes

PRESSURE BUILD:
25 minutes

PRESSURE COOK:
30 minutes, high

PRESSURE RELEASE:
Natural, 20 minutes

TOTAL TIME:
1 hour 45 minutes

1 (2-pound) beef brisket or beef chuck roast
2 teaspoons salt, divided
2 teaspoons neutral oil
1 sweet onion, chopped
4 garlic cloves, minced
4 cups beef broth or water
1 pound carrots, chopped

3 large potatoes, peeled and chopped
2 tablespoons tomato paste
2 teaspoons Chinese five-spice powder
2 teaspoons dried Valencia orange peel, or the peel of 1 fresh mandarin orange

1. Using a sharp knife, cut the beef brisket into 2-inch pieces, then place it in a large bowl. Sprinkle with 1 teaspoon of salt, mix, and set aside.

2. On the Instant Pot, select Sauté and adjust the heat to high to preheat the pot. Once hot, pour in the oil and add the onion. Stir-fry for about 2 minutes until soft. Add the garlic and stir-fry for about 30 seconds until fragrant.

3. Add the beef and sear for about 5 minutes, browning all sides.

4. Pour in the broth to deglaze the pot, scraping up any browned bits from the bottom. Add the carrots, potatoes, tomato paste, five-spice powder, and orange peel.

5. Lock the lid. Program to pressure cook (use Beef or Meat, if applicable) for 30 minutes on high pressure.

6. When the timer sounds, let the pressure release naturally for 20 minutes.

7. Carefully remove the lid. Stir the stew and it will thicken by itself as the sauce evaporates a bit. Serve.

SCALLION AND GINGER LAMB

This lamb stir-fry with scallion and ginger is seasoned lightly, so you can taste all the delicious flavors. After a quick stir-fry, the dish cooks very quickly under pressure, so the lamb is tender. The recipe calls for lamb shoulder, but you can also use about one-quarter of a boneless leg of lamb (and save the rest for other dishes).

SERVES 4

PREP TIME:
15 minutes

SAUTÉ:
5 minutes

PRESSURE BUILD:
5 minutes

PRESSURE COOK:
1 minute, high

PRESSURE RELEASE:
Quick

TOTAL TIME:
26 minutes

1 pound boneless lamb shoulder, cut into 1-inch cubes
1 tablespoon oyster sauce
1 tablespoon light soy sauce
3 teaspoons cornstarch, divided
1 teaspoon sugar
1 teaspoon rice wine
5 tablespoons water, divided

2 teaspoons neutral oil
½ sweet onion, sliced
2 garlic cloves, minced
1 (1-inch) piece fresh ginger, minced
4 scallions, white and green parts, chopped on the diagonal into 1-inch pieces
Cooked rice or noodles, for serving

1. In a large bowl, combine the lamb, oyster sauce, soy sauce, 1 teaspoon of cornstarch, the sugar, and wine. Mix, then set aside.

2. In a small bowl, whisk the remaining 2 teaspoons of cornstarch and 2 tablespoons of water. Set aside.

3. On the Instant Pot, select Sauté and adjust the heat to high to preheat the pot. Once hot, pour in the oil and add the onion, garlic, and ginger. Stir-fry for about 2 minutes until soft.

4. Spread the lamb evenly over the onion. Pour in the remaining 3 tablespoons of water and stir to deglaze.

5. Lock the lid. Program to pressure cook for 1 minute on high pressure.

6. When the timer sounds, quick release the pressure and carefully remove the lid.

7. Whisk the cornstarch slurry and stir it into the pot. Add the scallions. Cook, stirring with a clean utensil, until the sauce thickens and the lamb is cooked through. Serve with rice or noodles.

SPICY GARLIC CUMIN LAMB

Spicy cumin lamb is usually deep-fried, then stir-fried in a spicy sauce. This recipe includes all the flavors, but the meat is stir-fried and pressure cooked briefly, so it's cooked but tender.

SERVES 4

PREP TIME:
20 minutes

SAUTÉ:
5 minutes

PRESSURE BUILD:
5 minutes

PRESSURE COOK:
1 minute, high

PRESSURE RELEASE:
Quick

TOTAL TIME:
31 minutes

1 tablespoon cumin seeds or ground cumin

2 teaspoons whole or ground Sichuan peppercorns

1 teaspoon coriander seeds or ground coriander

1 pound boneless lamb shoulder or leg of lamb, cut into 1-inch cubes

1 tablespoon rice wine

1 teaspoon cornstarch

½ teaspoon salt

4 garlic cloves, minced

1 onion, diced

¼ cup water

2 tablespoons doubanjiang

1 tablespoon light soy sauce

2 teaspoons neutral oil

Cooked rice or noodles, for serving

1. If using whole spices, on the Instant Pot, select Sauté to preheat the pot. Once hot, place the cumin seeds, whole peppercorns, and coriander seeds in the pot and toast for 1 minute until fragrant. Transfer to a mortar and pestle and coarsely grind the spices. If using ground spices, combine the cumin, pepper, and coriander in a small bowl.

2. In a large bowl, combine the lamb, 2 teaspoons of the spice mix, wine, cornstarch, and salt and mix until thoroughly coated. Set aside.

3. Stir the garlic and onion into the remaining spices. Set aside.

4. In a small bowl, whisk the water, doubanjiang, and soy sauce and set aside.

5. Select Sauté again and adjust the heat to high to preheat the pot. Once hot, pour in the oil and add the garlic-onion spice mixture. Stir-fry for about 1 minute until fragrant. Add the lamb, spreading out the pieces.

6. Select Cancel. Pour in the soy sauce mixture and stir to loosen any stuck pieces of meat.

7. Lock the lid. Program to pressure cook for 1 minute on high pressure.

8. When the timer sounds, quick release the pressure. Carefully remove the lid and serve with rice or noodles.

INGREDIENT TIP: Doubanjiang is a fermented broad bean sauce from the Pixan region of Sichuan. There is a brown doubanjiang sauce that is sweet and a red doubanjiang sauce with chiles that's spicy. Different brands might be more or less spicy, so you might need to add chili oil depending on your preference. If you want to substitute something else for doubanjiang, use 1 tablespoon hoisin sauce and 1 tablespoon chili oil.

BRAISED LAMB AND VEGETABLE STEW

Lamb is generally very tender and cooks quickly compared to other red meats. Lamb shoulder chops have a little bit of everything that makes a great stew—bones for flavor, fat for satiety, and sinewy parts for texture. You can also use boneless leg of lamb.

SERVES 4

PREP TIME:
20 minutes

SAUTÉ:
15 minutes

**PRESSURE
BUILD:**
20 minutes

**PRESSURE
COOK:**
10 minutes,
high

**PRESSURE
RELEASE:**
Natural,
10 minutes

TOTAL TIME:
1 hour
15 minutes

2 pounds bone-in lamb
  shoulder chops
1 teaspoon salt
1 teaspoon freshly ground
  black pepper
3 teaspoons neutral oil, divided
1 onion, chopped
4 garlic cloves, smashed and peeled
1 (1-inch) piece fresh ginger,
  thinly sliced

6 carrots, chopped (2 cups)
6 celery stalks, chopped (2 cups)
2 tomatoes, cut into wedges
1 cup chicken or vegetable broth
  or water
2 tablespoons hoisin sauce, ensure
  gluten-free, if necessary
6 potatoes, peeled and chopped
  (2 cups)

1. Pat the lamb chops dry with paper towels and wipe away any loose bone fragments or bits of blood. Cut the meaty parts of the lamb chops into 1-inch cubes and leave some meat on the bones. Sprinkle the lamb pieces on both sides with the salt and pepper.

2. On the Instant Pot, select Sauté and adjust the heat to high to preheat the pot. Once hot, pour in 2 teaspoons of oil. Add half the lamb meat and bones and stir-fry for 2 minutes until browned. Transfer the browned lamb to a large bowl and repeat with the remaining lamb meat and bones.

3. Pour the remaining 1 teaspoon of oil into the pot and add the onion, garlic, and ginger. Stir-fry for 1 minute until fragrant. Add the carrots and celery and stir-fry for 1 minute.

4. Add the tomatoes, then pour in the broth and hoisin sauce to deglaze the pot, scraping any browned bits from the bottom. Add the potatoes and the browned meat and bones.

5. Lock the lid. Program to pressure cook on high pressure for 10 minutes.

6. When the timer sounds, let the pressure release naturally for 10 minutes, then quick release the remaining pressure. Remove the bones before serving.

VARIATION: The sauce is soupy and would be perfect served over a bowl of pasta or noodles. If you prefer to serve over rice and want a thicker sauce, remove the meat, then thicken the sauce with a cornstarch slurry.

STEAMED SPARERIBS WITH BLACK BEANS AND GARLIC

Steamed spareribs are a dim sum restaurant staple, where everyone has one or two morsels that leaves them wanting more. This family-size recipe is here to satisfy that craving. If we have leftovers, I reheat them with drained tofu cubes to round out our meal. Serve these ribs with rice and a favorite vegetable side dish.

SERVES 6

PREP TIME:
15 minutes, plus 15 minutes to marinate

PRESSURE BUILD:
10 minutes

PRESSURE COOK:
15 minutes, high

PRESSURE RELEASE:
Natural, 15 minutes

TOTAL TIME:
1 hour 10 minutes

1 tablespoon douchi (fermented black soybeans) or black bean and garlic sauce

3 garlic cloves, minced

2 teaspoons light soy sauce (use 1 teaspoon if using black bean and garlic sauce)

1 teaspoon rice wine

1 teaspoon sugar

2 pounds pork spareribs

2 teaspoons cornstarch

2 tablespoons water, plus 1 cup

1. If using whole douchi, rinse it with water, then chop it with the garlic. Transfer to a large bowl. If using black bean and garlic sauce, combine it with the minced garlic in a large bowl. Stir in the soy sauce, wine, and sugar. Set aside.

2. Pat the pork dry with paper towels, checking for any loose bone fragments, and cut the pork between each rib. Add the ribs to the sauce and mix to coat. Add the cornstarch and mix. Let marinate for 15 minutes, or overnight in the refrigerator, covered.

3. When ready to steam, transfer the ribs to a pressure-safe bowl, spread them out evenly and add 2 tablespoons of water.

4. Pour the remaining 1 cup of water into the Instant Pot and place a trivet inside. Place the bowl of ribs on the trivet.

5. Lock the lid. Program to pressure cook for 15 minutes on high pressure.

6. When the timer sounds, let the pressure release naturally for 15 minutes, then quick release the remaining pressure. The ribs are ready when there's a broth-like sauce in the pot. If there's not a broth-like sauce, the ribs may need to cook a little longer. Use a thermometer to ensure the ribs are 145°F.

INGREDIENT TIP: If you shop at a Chinese supermarket, you will find pork spareribs, baby back ribs, and pork riblets cut through the bone for this dish, or you can ask a butcher to cut a sparerib in half through the bones. I like pork spareribs because they're tasty, slightly leaner, and less bony. I also like cutting boneless country-style ribs into 1-inch cubes and pressure cooking them for 12 minutes. Prep a double batch and freeze the extra in a quart-size bag to save time. Thaw overnight in the refrigerator before pressure cooking.

STEAMED MINCED PORK WITH EGG

This recipe is a steamed meat patty made with hand-minced pork. There are egg-free variations of steamed minced pork. Instead of mixing in an egg, you can mix in minced shiitake mushrooms, minced salted preserved vegetables, or minced dried oysters. While steaming the pork, prep some Broccoli with Garlic (page 96) or Baby Bok Choy with Garlic and Ginger (page 92) to cook in the emptied and dried pot afterward and serve with rice.

SERVES 4

PREP TIME:
30 minutes

PRESSURE BUILD:
5 minutes

PRESSURE COOK:
10 minutes, high

PRESSURE RELEASE:
Natural, 5 minutes

TOTAL TIME:
50 minutes

1 pound boneless country-style pork ribs or pork butt
2 teaspoons light soy sauce
1 teaspoon sugar
1 teaspoon cornstarch
1 large egg, lightly beaten
1 cup water, plus 1 tablespoon, divided

1. Use a cleaver or chef's knife to dice the pork. Then, chop from left to right, fold the meat over, rotate it 90 degrees, and repeat until the pork is a fine mince. Transfer to a medium bowl. Stir in the soy sauce, sugar, and cornstarch. Add the egg and mix until combined. Transfer the pork to a pressure-safe bowl and smooth it down so it cooks evenly. Add 1 tablespoon of water to the bowl.

2. Pour the remaining 1 cup of water into the Instant Pot and place a trivet inside. Place the bowl of pork meat on the trivet.

3. Lock the lid. Program to pressure cook for 10 minutes on high pressure.

4. When the timer sounds, let the pressure release naturally for 5 minutes, then quick release the remaining pressure.

PREP TIP: This is a great recipe to try pot-in-pot cooking and save time by cooking two recipes at once. The recipe that takes more time to cook goes into the pot first and the recipe that cooks faster goes on top, wrapped with aluminum foil, if needed, to insulate the food from cooking too fast. Cook the minced pork on the bottom, add a second trivet, and steam vegetables on the top layer. Another option is to make rice in the pot (see Steamed White Rice variation, page 103) with the bowl of pork on a trivet.

SWEET-AND-SOUR SOY AND BLACK VINEGAR RIBS

I have called this dish "3-2-1 ribs" for as long as I can remember because that's how I memorized this soy-based sweet-and-sour recipe (3 spoons of sugar, 2 spoons of vinegar, 1 spoon of soy sauce). These ribs are a Cantonese interpretation of a Shanghai-style dish. The ribs are fried in melted and caramelized sugar, then braised with soy sauce and black vinegar. I have adapted the method and flavors for the Instant Pot.

SERVES 4

PREP TIME:
10 minutes

SAUTÉ:
10 minutes

PRESSURE BUILD:
30 minutes

PRESSURE COOK:
10 minutes, high

PRESSURE RELEASE:
Quick

TOTAL TIME:
1 hour

2½ pounds baby back spareribs
1 tablespoon rice wine
2 garlic cloves, chopped
1 teaspoon salt
3 tablespoons sugar

2 teaspoons neutral oil
½ cup water
2 tablespoons black vinegar
1 tablespoon light soy sauce

1. Pat the spareribs dry with paper towels and check for any bone fragments. Cut the ribs between each bone and place the pieces in a large bowl. Add the wine, garlic, and salt. Mix and set aside.

2. On the Instant Pot, select Sauté and adjust the heat to high. Pour the sugar and oil into the cold pot. Cook for 5 minutes, stirring constantly. The sugar will appear sandy, then pebbly. When the sugar melts and becomes tan colored, add the ribs and stir-fry for about 2 minutes to coat with the melted sugar and to brown.

3. Pour in the water, vinegar, and soy sauce to deglaze the pot, scraping up any browned bits from the bottom.

4. Lock the lid. Program to pressure cook for 10 minutes on high pressure.

5. When the timer sounds, quick release the pressure. The ribs are ready to serve as is. If you want them a bit crispy, brush some sauce on the ribs and broil them on a foil-lined baking sheet, watching carefully so they don't burn.

HONG SHAO ROU (RED COOKED PORK BELLY)

My friend Kristen urged me to include hong shao rou, which is the inspiration for this red braised pork belly recipe. *Hong shao* refers to a red braise technique that involves melting sugar in oil until the sugar caramelizes, which gives the meat a reddish color that is auspicious for celebrations. It is, indeed, good luck for me, as my father often talked about how he and his mom were able to survive on pork belly during hard times. Serve with rice and a vegetable side dish.

SERVES 6

PREP TIME:
15 minutes

SAUTÉ:
10 minutes

PRESSURE BUILD:
5 minutes

PRESSURE COOK:
15 minutes, high

PRESSURE RELEASE:
Natural, 10 minutes

TOTAL TIME:
55 minutes

2½ pounds skin-on pork belly, cut into 2-inch pieces

4½ cups water, divided

1 teaspoon neutral oil

3 tablespoons sugar

2 tablespoons rice wine

2 tablespoons dark soy sauce

1 tablespoon light soy sauce

1 (½-inch) piece fresh ginger, thinly sliced

2 star anise pods

1. Place the pork in the Instant Pot and pour in 4 cups of water. Select Sauté and adjust the heat to high. Let the water come to a boil and boil the pork belly for 1 to 2 minutes. There will be some foam and impurities that rise to the surface.

2. Drain and rinse the pork in a colander and pat dry with paper towels. Clean and dry the liner and return it to the base.

3. Select Sauté again and pour in the oil and sugar, then add the pork belly. Stir-fry the pork for 5 minutes until it browns.

4. Pour in the wine and stir-fry for 1 minute. Pour in the remaining ½ cup of water to deglaze the pot, scraping up any browned bits from the bottom.

5. Add the dark and light soy sauces, ginger, and star anise.

6. Lock the lid. Program to pressure cook for 15 minutes on high pressure.

7. When the timer sounds, let the pressure release naturally for 10 minutes, then quick release the remaining pressure.

8. Carefully remove the lid, select Sauté again, and adjust the heat to low. Simmer for about 5 minutes, stirring occasionally, until the liquid is reduced.

VARIATION: You can add a few cooked and peeled hard-boiled eggs and sauté on low for a few minutes to braise the eggs and to thicken the sauce. Remove all but ¼ cup of sauce, add ½ cup water and 1 pound bok choy and pressure cook for 0 minutes with a quick pressure release.

LU RAO FAN (BRAISED PORK AND EGG RICE BOWL)

This braised pork and egg rice bowl is a Taiwanese favorite. It's typically made with soft, succulent pork belly and enjoyed as one of several dishes in a big meal. In this recipe, I use pork butt, which is a leaner cut but still fall-apart tender after pressure cooking and ready to eat (instead of chilling overnight to remove the extra fat from the sauce). I add the peeled eggs to the pot at the end of pressure cooking, so they warm in the residual heat and soak in all the wonderful flavors without becoming overcooked.

SERVES 6

PREP TIME:
20 minutes, plus 10 minutes to soak

SAUTÉ:
15 minutes

PRESSURE BUILD:
10 minutes

PRESSURE COOK:
25 minutes, high

PRESSURE RELEASE:
Quick

TOTAL TIME:
1 hour 20 minutes

1 cup water, divided

6 large eggs

3 tablespoons neutral oil

2 shallots, sliced

4 garlic cloves, sliced

1 (1-inch) piece fresh ginger, thinly sliced

2 pounds pork shoulder or pork belly, cut into 2- to 3-inch pieces

2 tablespoons rice wine

2 tablespoons dark soy sauce

1 tablespoon light soy sauce

2 tablespoons sugar, or 30 grams rock sugar

½ teaspoon Chinese five-spice powder

2¼ cups cooked medium- or long-grain white rice

1. Prepare an ice bath and set aside.

2. Pour ½ cup of water into the Instant Pot, place a trivet inside, and put the eggs on it. Program to pressure cook for 5 minutes on high pressure.

3. When the timer sounds, quick release the pressure and transfer the eggs to the ice bath. Empty and dry the liner before returning it to the base.

4. On the Instant Pot, select Sauté and adjust the heat to high to preheat the pot. Once hot, pour in the oil and add the shallots. Stir-fry for about 5 minutes until the shallots are browned. Use a slotted spoon to transfer the shallots to a small bowl, leaving the oil in the pot.

5. Add the garlic and ginger to the pot and stir-fry for about 1 minute until fragrant.

6. Add the pork and stir-fry for about 2 minutes until browned.

7. Pour in the wine to deglaze the pot, scraping up any browned bits from the bottom.

8. Pour in the dark and light soy sauces, the remaining ½ cup of water, and the sugar. Add the five-spice powder and half of the shallots.

9. Lock the lid. Program to pressure cook for 20 minutes on high pressure.

10. While the pork cooks, peel the eggs.

11. When the timer sounds, quick release the pressure, select Cancel, and then select Keep Warm.

12. Carefully remove the lid, add the eggs, lock the lid again, and let the eggs soak for 10 minutes.

13. Serve a scoop of braised pork over rice. Halve an egg and arrange it next to the pork, then top with a spoonful of fried shallots and a drizzle of braising sauce.

VARIATION: Reserve any leftover sauce to use as a brown stir-fry sauce for other dishes. Boil it for a few minutes, strain, and refrigerate.

CHAPTER FIVE

POULTRY AND SEAFOOD

Soy-Braised Duck Legs with Ginger and Scallions,
page 72

SOY-BRAISED DUCK LEGS WITH GINGER AND SCALLIONS

This recipe is an Instant Pot adaptation of *luo shui ya*, which is duck braised with soy sauce, aromatics, and five-spice or master sauce (see page 6). The advantage of pressure cooking duck legs is that the duck legs cook faster and more evenly than a whole duck.

SERVES 4

PREP TIME:
10 minutes

SAUTÉ:
15 minutes

PRESSURE BUILD:
5 minutes

PRESSURE COOK:
20 minutes, high

PRESSURE RELEASE:
Natural, 5 minutes

TOTAL TIME:
55 minutes

4 duck legs, thawed if frozen

½ teaspoon salt

1 (1-inch) piece fresh ginger, thinly sliced

2 tablespoons rice wine

3 scallions, trimmed and halved

2 tablespoons dark soy sauce

1 tablespoon light soy sauce

1 tablespoon sugar

½ cup water

Cooked rice, for serving (optional)

1. Use scissors to trim off any excess duck fat and skin and reserve. Pat the duck legs dry with paper towels and sprinkle the meat side with the salt.

2. On the Instant Pot, select Sauté and adjust the heat to high. Add the duck fat and duck skin pieces—they should sizzle within a minute. Stir frequently until they render enough fat to cover the bottom of the pot and the control panel indicates Hot.

3. Place 2 duck legs in the pot, skin-side down, and sear for 3 minutes. Flip and sear the other side for 2 minutes. Remove and repeat with the remaining 2 duck legs.

4. Select Cancel. Remove the legs and pour the excess duck fat into a small storage container or jar to reserve for other uses.

5. Place the liner back into the base. Add the ginger and pour in the wine to deglaze the pot, scraping up any browned bits from the bottom.

6. Add the scallions and place the duck legs on top. Pour in the dark and light soy sauces, sugar, and water.

7. Lock the lid. Program to pressure cook for 20 minutes on high pressure.

8. When the timer sounds, let the pressure release naturally for 5 minutes, then quick release the remaining pressure. Serve as is, or with rice.

CHICKEN THIGHS AND BEAN SPROUTS WITH OYSTER SAUCE

This recipe might remind you of chicken chow fun but without the stir-fried rice noodles. The chicken is juicy and tender, the bean sprouts have a little bit of crunch, and the oyster sauce ties it all together in a dish that can be enjoyed over rice. Untrimmed bean sprouts taste fine, but trimmed sprouts look better in the final dish.

SERVES 6

PREP TIME:
20 minutes

SAUTÉ:
5 minutes

PRESSURE BUILD:
10 minutes

PRESSURE COOK:
2 minutes, high

PRESSURE RELEASE:
Quick

TOTAL TIME:
37 minutes

1¼ pounds boneless, skinless chicken thighs (6 or 7 thighs)
2 tablespoons oyster sauce, divided
2 teaspoons light soy sauce, divided
1 teaspoon sugar
2 teaspoons cornstarch
2 tablespoons water, plus ¼ cup, divided

2 teaspoons neutral oil
½ sweet onion, sliced
1 garlic clove, minced
1 (12-ounce) package mung bean sprouts, rinsed and ends trimmed
1 scallion, white and green parts, thinly sliced

1. Cut each chicken thigh into 3 or 4 equal pieces and place them in a large bowl. Add 1 tablespoon of oyster sauce, 1 teaspoon of soy sauce, and the sugar. Mix and set aside.

2. In a small bowl, whisk the remaining 1 tablespoon of oyster sauce, remaining 1 teaspoon of soy sauce, cornstarch, and 2 tablespoons of water. Set aside.

3. On the Instant Pot, select Sauté and adjust the heat to high to preheat the pot. Once hot, pour in the oil and add the chicken, spreading it out to sear. Cook for 1 minute until browned. Add the onion and garlic and stir-fry for 1 minute until slightly softened and fragrant. Pour in the remaining ¼ cup of water.

4. Lock the lid. Program to pressure cook for 2 minutes on high pressure.

5. When the timer sounds, quick release the pressure.

6. Carefully remove the lid. Whisk the cornstarch slurry and add it to the pot, along with the bean sprouts and scallion. Gently fold the sprouts in. Lock the lid and let cook in the residual heat for 2 to 3 minutes.

INGREDIENT TIP: Mung bean sprouts are often sold alongside soybean sprouts and they look similar. Mung bean sprouts have a creamy white color and soybean sprouts look yellowish-white and have a few yellow soybeans in the bag. Trim the sprouts by removing the straggly tails.

CHICKEN LEG QUARTERS WITH GINGER-SCALLION SAUCE

This recipe is inspired by Hainan chicken and rice, which is poached chicken served with flavored rice and a trio of dipping sauces. I've adapted the recipe for the Instant Pot, using chicken leg quarters instead of a whole chicken. Because the chicken is served warm or at room temperature, it's perfect on a hot day with sliced cucumbers, tomato wedges, or a small salad. It's your choice whether to make the rice first and keep it warm while cooking the chicken or vice versa.

SERVES 4

PREP TIME:
15 minutes

SAUTÉ:
4 minutes

PRESSURE BUILD:
20 minutes

PRESSURE COOK:
8 minutes, high

PRESSURE RELEASE:
Natural, 5 minutes

TOTAL TIME:
52 minutes

FOR THE GINGER-SCALLION SAUCE

1 (1-inch) piece fresh ginger, thinly sliced
2 scallions, white and green parts, thinly sliced
2 tablespoons neutral oil
¼ teaspoon salt

FOR THE CHICKEN

1 (1-inch) piece fresh ginger, thinly sliced
2 scallions, white and green parts, torn in half
4 chicken leg quarters
2 teaspoons salt
2½ cups Chicken Stock with Ginger (page 32) or store-bought chicken broth
1 tablespoon rice wine
1 recipe Steamed White Rice (page 103) or Chicken and Garlic Shallot Rice (page 104)
Cucumber slices, for serving

TO MAKE THE GINGER-SCALLION SAUCE

1. Mince the ginger and scallions together.

2. On the Instant Pot, select Sauté and adjust the heat to high to preheat the pot. Once hot, pour in the oil and add the minced ginger and scallions and salt. Stir-fry for about 1 minute until fragrant. Select Cancel. Transfer the sauce to a small serving bowl.

TO MAKE THE CHICKEN

3. Place the ginger and scallions in the pot.

4. Rub the chicken legs with the salt and use paper towels to pat them and remove the excess salt. Arrange the chicken legs in a single layer in the pot and pour in the stock and wine.

5. Lock the lid. Program to pressure cook for 8 minutes on high pressure. Meanwhile, fill a large bowl halfway with cold water.

6. When the timer sounds, let the pressure release naturally for 5 minutes, then quick release the remaining pressure. Carefully remove the lid.

7. Use tongs to transfer the chicken to the water bath for 5 minutes. Drain the water from the chicken.

8. Serve the chicken with a spoonful of ginger-scallion sauce on top, and on the side, a scoop of rice and cucumber slices.

9. Strain and save the chicken cooking liquid as stock for other recipes. It will be very concentrated and salty.

FIVE-SPICE AND SOY SAUCE CHICKEN DRUMSTICKS

My dad taught me how to cook a five-spice soy sauce–braised whole chicken, which is a master sauce recipe and technique he learned while working in San Francisco's Chinatown. It's a versatile recipe that I've adapted for cooking in the Instant Pot, using chicken drumsticks, which are much easier and faster to cook. Serve with rice and a vegetable side dish

SERVES 6

PREP TIME:
10 minutes

PRESSURE BUILD:
15 minutes

PRESSURE COOK:
8 minutes, high

PRESSURE RELEASE:
Natural, 5 minutes

TOTAL TIME:
38 minutes

1 cup water
½ cup light soy sauce
12 chicken drumsticks
3 scallions, trimmed and halved
6 garlic cloves, coarsely chopped
1 (1-inch) piece fresh ginger, thinly sliced
2 tablespoons brown sugar
1 teaspoon Chinese five-spice powder

1. In the Instant Pot, stir together the water, soy sauce, chicken, scallions, garlic, ginger, brown sugar, and five-spice powder. Arrange the chicken in one layer.

2. Lock the lid. Program to pressure cook for 8 minutes on high pressure.

3. When the timer sounds, let the pressure release naturally for 5 minutes, then quick release the remaining pressure.

PREP TIP: Master sauce is also known as *lu shui zhi*. Save the sauce here for the next time you make any five-spice soy-braised dish. If I know I will reuse it within a week, I strain and save the sauce in a clean sturdy jar. Otherwise, freeze the master sauce in a freezer-safe container. If you want to cook another batch of drumsticks, combine the chicken, master sauce, fresh aromatics, and consider adding more salt, sugar, and five-spice powder.

GARLIC-SOY CHICKEN OVER RICE

Bo zai fan is a cooking style in which raw rice is topped with marinated meats and Chinese sausages, then cooked together in a clay pot. As the rice simmers, the steam cooks the meat, which flavors the rice. I have adapted the recipe for cooking in an Instant Pot. The recipe requires very little hands-on time and, while you're waiting for the chicken to marinate, you can prep a bowl of Steamed Mixed Vegetables (page 97).

SERVES 4

PREP TIME:
20 minutes

PRESSURE BUILD:
10 minutes

PRESSURE COOK:
4 minutes, high

PRESSURE RELEASE:
Natural, 10 minutes

TOTAL TIME:
44 minutes

12 ounces boneless, skinless chicken thighs, cut into 2 or 3 pieces

2 teaspoons light soy sauce

1 teaspoon sesame oil

2 garlic cloves, minced

2 scallions, white and green parts, thinly sliced, divided

1½ cups long-grain or jasmine white rice

1½ cups water

2 lap cheong (Chinese sausages), cut into ¼-inch slices

1 teaspoon toasted sesame seeds

1. In a large bowl, mix the chicken, soy sauce, sesame oil, garlic, and half the scallions. Let marinate for 15 minutes.

2. In a medium bowl, rinse and drain the rice two times, then pour it into the Instant Pot. Pour in the water and use a spoon to level the rice. Arrange the chicken and lap cheong on the rice.

3. Lock the lid. Program to pressure cook for 4 minutes on high pressure.

4. When the timer sounds, let the pressure release naturally for 10 minutes, then quick release the remaining pressure.

5. Serve the chicken, lap cheong, and rice sprinkled with the remaining scallion and the sesame seeds.

SWEET-AND-TANGY CHICKEN THIGHS WITH PINEAPPLE

Whenever I eat sweet-and-sour pork, my favorite part is the pineapple coated with a sweet-and-tangy sauce. Here, we use the Instant Pot to capture all the flavors of a sweet-and-sour sauce with pineapple, chicken thighs, and bell peppers, in a hearty meal for busy weeknights.

SERVES 4

PREP TIME:
10 minutes

SAUTÉ:
20 minutes

PRESSURE BUILD:
10 minutes

PRESSURE COOK:
8 minutes, high

PRESSURE RELEASE:
Natural, 5 minutes

TOTAL TIME:
53 minutes

2 pounds bone-in, skin-on chicken thighs (6 to 8 pieces)
½ teaspoon salt
1 (20-ounce) can pineapple chunks in juice
1 onion, chopped

¼ cup ketchup
¼ cup rice vinegar
¼ cup sugar
1 red bell pepper, chopped
Cooked rice, for serving

1. Season the chicken thighs with salt and set aside.

2. Drain the pineapples over a large measuring cup, reserving ¼ cup juice and the pineapple.

3. On the Instant Pot, select Sauté and adjust the heat to high to preheat the pot. Once hot, place half the chicken thighs, skin-side down, in the pot. Cook for about 3 minutes to brown and render some fat. When the chicken releases easily, brown the other side for 3 minutes. Remove and repeat with the remaining thighs.

4. Add the onion and stir-fry for about 2 minutes until softened and browned slightly. Pour in the reserved pineapple juice to deglaze the pot, scraping up any browned bits from the bottom. Select Cancel.

5. Stir in the ketchup, vinegar, and sugar. Add the chicken pieces, skin-side up, and half the pineapple pieces.

6. Lock the lid. Program to pressure cook for 8 minutes on high pressure.

7. When the timer sounds, let the pressure release naturally for 5 minutes, then quick release the remaining pressure.

8. Carefully remove the lid and use tongs to transfer the chicken pieces to a serving platter.

9. Select Sauté again. Cook the sauce until it is bubbly, then add the bell pepper. Cook for about 2 minutes, or until the sauce is slightly reduced and the pepper is crisp-tender. Ladle the bell peppers and sauce over the chicken and garnish with the remaining pineapple on the side.

10. Serve with rice.

VARIATION: This recipe is highly adaptable to cook with tofu or shrimp instead of chicken. Drain and/or dry the tofu or shrimp, then use the Sauté function to brown before pressure cooking for 0 minutes, or 1 minute. The bell pepper can be cooked at the same time.

EASY LEMON CHICKEN

Usually, lemon chicken is deep-fried and coated with a sweet sauce. This variation has all the flavors but is prepared as a simple stir-fry. Serve with Steamed Mixed Vegetables (page 97) or Baby Bok Choy with Garlic and Ginger (page 92).

SERVES 4

PREP TIME:
15 minutes

SAUTÉ:
15 minutes

PRESSURE BUILD:
5 minutes

PRESSURE COOK:
2 minutes, high

PRESSURE RELEASE:
Quick

TOTAL TIME:
37 minutes

2 boneless, skinless chicken breasts
1 large egg white, lightly beaten
2 tablespoons light soy sauce, divided
4 tablespoons sugar, divided
6 tablespoons cornstarch, divided

2 tablespoons freshly squeezed lemon juice
1 tablespoon garlic chili sauce
¼ cup water, plus 2 tablespoons, divided
2 teaspoons neutral oil
½ onion, chopped

1. Cut the chicken into 2-by-1-inch pieces and place them in a large bowl. Add the egg white, 1 tablespoon of soy sauce, and 1 tablespoon of sugar and mix. Add 4 tablespoons of cornstarch, mix again, and set aside.

2. In a small bowl, whisk the remaining 1 tablespoon of soy sauce, remaining 3 tablespoons of sugar, lemon juice, garlic chili sauce, and ¼ cup of water to combine.

3. In a second small bowl, whisk the remaining 2 tablespoons of cornstarch with the remaining 2 tablespoons of water. Set aside.

4. On the Instant Pot, select Sauté and adjust the heat to high to preheat the pot. Once hot, pour in the oil and add the chicken, spreading it out to sear. Cook for 1 minute, then stir-fry for about 1 minute more until browned on both sides.

5. Add the onion and soy–lemon juice mixture and stir to deglaze the pot, scraping up any browned bits from the bottom.

6. Lock the lid and program to pressure cook for 2 minutes on high pressure. When the timer sounds, quick release the pressure. Carefully remove the lid. Select Sauté again.

7. Whisk the cornstarch slurry and add it to the pot. Cook, stirring, for about 2 minutes until the sauce bubbles and thickens slightly.

CURRY SHRIMP AND VEGETABLE SPAGHETTI

This recipe is inspired by a dish called Singapore *chow mei fun* (stir-fried curried rice vermicelli), which was invented in the 1950s by Hong Kong chefs working at *cha chaan tengs* (Hong Kong cafes). The recipe became so popular, it's still on Chinese restaurant menus 70 years later. Rice vermicelli tends to stick to the Instant Pot, so I adapted the recipe to use spaghetti. Serve with a salad or steamed vegetables.

SERVES 4

PREP TIME:
5 minutes

SAUTÉ:
9 minutes

PRESSURE BUILD:
3 minutes

PRESSURE COOK:
5 minutes, high

PRESSURE RELEASE:
Natural, 5 minutes

TOTAL TIME:
27 minutes

4 teaspoons neutral oil, divided

2 large eggs, lightly beaten

½ onion, sliced

8 ounces small shrimp, peeled and deveined

1 celery stalk, thinly sliced on the diagonal

½ red bell pepper, julienned

2 cups water

2 teaspoons light soy sauce

2 teaspoons curry powder

8 ounces spaghetti

⅛ teaspoon freshly ground black pepper

1. On the Instant Pot, select Sauté and adjust the heat to high to preheat the pot. Once hot, pour in 2 teaspoons of oil, spread it to coat the bottom of the pot, and add the eggs. Cook, stirring for about 1 minute, until cooked. Transfer to a large bowl.

2. Pour the remaining 2 teaspoons of oil into the pot and add the onion. Stir-fry for 1 minute until lightly browned.

3. Add the shrimp and stir-fry for 2 minutes. Add the celery and bell pepper and stir-fry for 1 minute until crisp-tender. Scoop the shrimp and vegetables into the egg bowl.

4. In the pot, combine the water, soy sauce, and curry powder to deglaze the pot, scraping up any browned bits from the bottom. Break the spaghetti in half, add to the pot, and stir.

5. Lock the lid. Program to pressure cook for 5 minutes on high pressure. When the timer sounds, release the pressure naturally for 5 minutes, then quick release the remaining pressure.

6. Carefully remove the lid. Sprinkle in the pepper and stir in the shrimp, vegetables, and egg.

SHRIMP, EGG, AND BROCCOLINI RICE

My husband's family loves Fujian fried rice, a simple fried rice that's topped with a seafood and egg sauce and thinly sliced *gai lan* (Chinese broccoli) stems. This Instant Pot adaptation combines the flavors and texture of Fujian fried rice with freshly cooked rice.

SERVES 4

PREP TIME:
15 minutes

SAUTÉ:
10 minutes

PRESSURE BUILD:
10 minutes

PRESSURE COOK:
12 minutes, high

PRESSURE RELEASE:
Natural, 10 minutes

TOTAL TIME:
57 minutes

2½ cups water, divided
1½ cups white rice (jasmine, medium- or long-grain), rinsed
4 teaspoons neutral oil, divided
1 large egg, lightly beaten
2 garlic cloves, minced
1 carrot, diced
1 pound medium shrimp, peeled and deveined

4 broccolini or gai lan stems, thinly sliced
2 tablespoons oyster sauce
1 teaspoon light soy sauce
1 cup chicken or vegetable broth
1 tablespoon cornstarch

1. Pour 1 of cup water into the Instant Pot and place a trivet inside.

2. In a pressure-proof bowl, stir together the remaining 1½ cups of water, rice, and 1 teaspoon of oil. Place the bowl on the trivet.

3. Lock the lid. Program to pressure cook for 12 minutes on high pressure.

4. When the timer sounds, let the pressure release naturally for 10 minutes, then quick release the remaining pressure. Transfer the rice to a large serving bowl. Cover with a lid or aluminum foil to keep warm. Empty and dry the liner before returning it to the base.

5. Select Sauté and adjust the heat to high to preheat the pot. Once hot, pour in 2 teaspoons of oil and use a silicone spatula to coat the bottom of the pot with it. Add the egg and cook for about 1 minute until scrambled. Transfer the scrambled egg to the rice and keep warm.

6. Pour the remaining 1 teaspoon of oil into the pot. Add the garlic and carrot. Stir-fry for 1 minute until fragrant. Add the shrimp and stir-fry for 1 minute. Stir in the broccolini, oyster sauce, and soy sauce.

7. In a small bowl, whisk the broth and cornstarch, then add it to the pot. Cook for about 1 minute until the sauce bubbles and thickens.

8. Meanwhile, fluff the rice and incorporate the egg.

9. Pour the sauce over the rice and serve.

SHRIMP AND ASPARAGUS STIR-FRY

Shrimp and asparagus pair well because of their similar cooking times. A splash of rice wine flash-cooks the shrimp with a burst of steam and allows the alcohol to evaporate while flavoring the shrimp. Asparagus stalks that are thicker in width are preferable, but cut them on the diagonal, so they are less fibrous. You could also use snap peas or chopped bok choy instead of asparagus.

SERVES 4

PREP TIME:
15 minutes

SAUTÉ:
8 minutes

TOTAL TIME:
23 minutes

1 pound large (16 to 20 count) shrimp, peeled with last section and tail left on, and deveined
½ teaspoon salt
¼ teaspoon ground white pepper
1 tablespoon cornstarch
2 teaspoons neutral oil
2 garlic cloves, minced

1 tablespoon rice wine
⅓ cup water
1 pound asparagus, woody ends trimmed, cut on the diagonal into bite-size pieces
Cooked white rice or noodles, for serving (optional)

1. Pat the shrimp dry with paper towels and place in a medium bowl. Sprinkle with the salt and pepper and mix. Add the cornstarch and mix again. Set aside.

2. On the Instant Pot, select Sauté and adjust the heat to high to preheat the pot. Once hot, pour in the oil and add the garlic. Stir-fry for about 30 seconds until fragrant.

3. Add the shrimp and spread them out. Sear for 1 minute, then stir-fry for 1 minute. Pour in the wine and stir-fry for 30 seconds. Transfer the shrimp to a clean bowl.

4. Pour the water into the pot and add the asparagus. Stir-fry for 2 minutes until the asparagus is bright green. Return the shrimp to the pot and stir to combine and heat through for about 2 minutes. Serve as is, or with rice or noodles (if desired).

INGREDIENT TIP: I save shrimp shells in a small zip bag and freeze them for later use. For extra flavor, cook in broth or water for 5 minutes, discard the shells, then use the liquid in Scallop, Shrimp, and Crab Soup (page 42) or Wontons with Chicken and Pork Stock (page 26).

SEAFOOD PASTA

This recipe is inspired by Chinese lobster *yee mein*, which is stir-fried fresh lobster over fresh Chinese noodles. Using frozen mixed seafood and dried spaghetti in the Instant Pot optimizes the recipe for convenience, cost, and time for a quick and easy meal.

SERVES 6

PREP TIME:
15 minutes

SAUTÉ:
10 minutes

PRESSURE BUILD:
15 minutes

PRESSURE COOK:
5 minutes, high

PRESSURE RELEASE:
Natural, 5 minutes

TOTAL TIME:
50 minutes

2 pounds frozen seafood mix, thawed and drained

2 teaspoons cornstarch

2 tablespoons oyster sauce

4 teaspoons light soy sauce, divided

⅛ teaspoon ground white pepper

1 tablespoon neutral oil

4 garlic cloves, minced

1 (1-inch) piece fresh ginger, thinly sliced

2 scallions, white and green parts, chopped, divided

1 tablespoon rice wine

2 cups water, divided

1 pound spaghetti

1. Rinse and pat the seafood mix dry with a paper towel and place it in a large bowl. Toss with the cornstarch and set aside.

2. In a small bowl, whisk the oyster sauce, 2 teaspoons of soy sauce, and pepper. Set aside.

3. On the Instant Pot, select Sauté and adjust the heat to high to preheat the pot. Once hot, pour in the oil and add the garlic, ginger, and half the scallions. Stir-fry for 1 minute until fragrant.

4. Add the seafood and stir-fry for 2 minutes until the pot is sizzling again. Pour in the wine and stir for 30 seconds. Pour in the oyster sauce mixture and stir-fry for 1 minute. Select Cancel. Transfer the seafood to a clean bowl.

5. Pour in 1 cup of water to deglaze the pot, scraping up any browned bits from the bottom. Break the spaghetti in half and put it in the pot. Pour in the remaining 1 cup of water.

6. Lock the lid. Program to pressure cook for 5 minutes on high pressure. When the timer sounds, let the pressure release naturally for 5 minutes, then quick release the remaining pressure. Carefully remove the lid, stir the pasta, and add the remaining scallions and the seafood. Let warm for a minute, then serve.

STEAMED WHOLE FISH WITH GINGER AND SCALLIONS

You can taste the flavors and freshness of fish when it's cooked Chinese style. Therefore, it is essential to source the freshest fish for this recipe, which is steamed and seasoned with ginger, scallions, and a light drizzle of soy sauce. Asian markets have tanks of fresh fish still swimming at the time of purchase. My favorite is called *mang cho*, a fish often labeled "black bass." Otherwise, look for fish that have bright clear eyes, vivid red gills, and shiny firm skin. Ask the fishmonger to gut and clean the fish. A fish or a fish steak that is about 1 pound (1¼ pounds max) will fit in a pressure-safe container inside the Instant Pot and serves 4 people.

SERVES 4

PREP TIME:
10 minutes

PRESSURE BUILD:
5 minutes

PRESSURE COOK:
9 minutes, high

PRESSURE RELEASE:
Quick or Natural, depending on the fish weight, 5 minutes

TOTAL TIME:
29 minutes

1 (1-pound) whole fresh fish (black bass, black cod, rock cod)

2 scallions, green and white parts, julienned on the diagonal

1 (1-inch) piece fresh ginger, julienned

2 tablespoons water, plus 1 cup

2 teaspoons light soy sauce

Cooked rice or rice porridge, for serving

1. If the fish needs additional cleaning, use a paring knife to scale the fish, and use a knife or scissors to cut off any remnants of the gills. Clean the inside of the fish, drain, then pat dry with paper towels.

2. Arrange the fish in a pressure-safe bowl. Place the scallions and ginger on top, then add 2 tablespoons of water to the bowl.

3. Pour the remaining 1 cup of water into the Instant Pot and place a trivet inside. Place the bowl of fish on the trivet.

4. Lock the lid. Program to pressure cook for 9 minutes on high pressure.

5. If the fish weighs 1 to 1.1 pounds, quick release the pressure. If the fish weighs 1.1 to 1.25 pounds, let the pressure release naturally for 5 minutes, then quick release the remaining pressure.

6. Drizzle with soy sauce.

7. To serve, use one or two large serving spoons to scoop large pieces of the fish along the spine; check for small bones. Enjoy with rice or rice porridge.

INGREDIENT TIP: You can also steam fillets, but they must be very fresh and not have any fishy odor. Adjust the cook time depending on the thickness of the fillets. Sole fillets are very thin and will cook fast (6 to 7 minutes), whereas Chilean sea bass or salmon steaks are thicker with a big bone and will need a few more minutes (10 to 11 minutes).

VARIATION TIP: Drizzle with coconut aminos for a soy-free option or tamari sauce for a gluten-free option.

CHAPTER SIX

VEGETABLES AND RICE

Baby Bok Choy with Garlic and Ginger, page 92

BABY BOK CHOY WITH GARLIC AND GINGER

Baby bok choy is harvested early, when it's 3 to 5 inches tall. Baby bok choy has creamy white stalks and dark-green frilly leaves. Sometimes, you might see baby bok choy that's green with smooth flat leaves, which is actually Shanghai bok choy. Both varieties can be cooked the same way. For this recipe, the bok choy will finish cooking within 2 to 3 minutes after you put the lid on but before the Instant Pot builds up enough pressure to seal. If only mature bok choy is available, chop it into 2-inch pieces.

SERVES 4

PREP TIME:
10 minutes

SAUTÉ:
5 minutes

PRESSURE BUILD:
2 minutes

PRESSURE COOK:
0 minutes, high

TOTAL TIME:
17 minutes

12 ounces baby bok choy

1 teaspoon neutral oil

1 (½-inch) piece fresh ginger, julienned

2 garlic cloves, chopped

⅛ teaspoon salt

¼ cup water or vegetable broth

1 teaspoon oyster sauce, sesame oil, or soy sauce (optional)

1. Cut off a thin slice from the bottom of the bok choy stems, then separate 4 or 5 of the leaves. Halve the remaining bok choy lengthwise.

2. On the Instant Pot, select Sauté and adjust the heat to high. Preheat for 3 minutes.

3. Pour the oil into the Instant Pot and add the ginger and garlic. Stir-fry for 1 minute until fragrant.

4. Sprinkle the salt into the pot and add the bok choy. Stir-fry for 1 minute. Pour in the water.

5. Lock the lid. Program to pressure cook for 0 minutes (or 1 minute) on high pressure.

6. Set a timer for 2 minutes. When it sounds, carefully remove the lid to check for doneness. The bok choy should look more vivid in color and taste crisp-tender. Depending on the size of your bok choy, cook for another 30 seconds.

7. Stir in the oyster sauce (if using). Immediately transfer the bok choy to a plate so it doesn't overcook.

ICEBERG LETTUCE WITH OYSTER SAUCE

Many Chinese American families have iceberg lettuce on display as an ancestral offering around Lunar New Year. *Shengcai*, the Chinese word for lettuce, sounds like "wealth" in Chinese and is considered auspicious and lucky. Cooking iceberg lettuce in the Instant Pot preserves the nutritional value of the lettuce and is so easy compared to other cooking methods. You can also make this recipe with romaine lettuce. The lettuce will finish cooking after you put the lid on but before the Instant Pot builds up enough pressure to seal.

SERVES 4

PREP TIME:
5 minutes

PRESSURE BUILD:
5 minutes

PRESSURE COOK:
0 minutes, high

TOTAL TIME:
10 minutes

½ cup water

2 teaspoons oyster sauce

1 teaspoon neutral oil

1 head iceberg lettuce

1. Pour the water, oyster sauce, and oil into the Instant Pot.

2. Tear the iceberg lettuce leaves into pieces about the size of your hand and place them in the pot, pushing the leaves down so they are no higher than the max fill line.

3. Lock the lid. Program to pressure cook for 0 minutes on high pressure (or 1 minute, depending on your model).

4. Set a timer for 5 minutes. When it sounds, quick release the pressure and carefully remove the lid and check for doneness. The lettuce should be wilted slightly. Use tongs to stir the lettuce, so the lettuce that is on top goes underneath. Select Cancel. Transfer the lettuce to a serving bowl.

VARIATION TIP: One of my favorite condiments is oyster sauce and I use it for everything. For those who prefer a shellfish-free option or a vegan option, consider using a mushroom "oyster" sauce.

SOY-BRAISED MUSHROOMS WITH ICEBERG LETTUCE

This dish is often served as a vegetable course at Chinese banquets for weddings, milestone birthdays, and other celebratory events. The mushrooms are served on a bed of cooked Chinese vegetables and, sometimes, with seafood.

SERVES 4

PREP TIME:
15 minutes, plus 30 minutes to soak

SAUTÉ:
5 minutes

PRESSURE BUILD:
15 minutes

PRESSURE COOK:
25 minutes, high

PRESSURE RELEASE:
Natural, 5 minutes

TOTAL TIME:
1 hour 35 minutes

12 dried shiitake mushrooms

1 teaspoon neutral oil

1 (½-inch) piece fresh ginger, thinly sliced

2 garlic cloves, chopped

1 tablespoon oyster sauce

2 teaspoons light soy sauce

2 teaspoons sugar

1 head iceberg lettuce, leaves torn into about 5-inch pieces

1. In a medium bowl, rinse the mushrooms, then add enough water to cover. Weight the mushrooms with another bowl of water to keep them submerged. Soak for 30 minutes, or until soft.

2. Use kitchen scissors to remove the mushroom stems and discard. Squeeze the excess water from the mushrooms back into the bowl.

3. Use a tea strainer or cheesecloth to filter and reserve 1 cup of the mushroom soaking water.

4. On the Instant Pot, select Sauté to preheat the pot. Once hot, pour in the oil and add the ginger and garlic. Stir-fry for 1 minute until fragrant.

5. Add the mushrooms, the reserved mushroom soaking water, oyster sauce, soy sauce, and sugar and stir.

6. Lock the lid. Program to pressure cook for 20 minutes on high pressure.

7. When the timer sounds, let the pressure release naturally for 5 minutes, then quick release the remaining pressure.

8. Using a slotted spoon, transfer the mushrooms to another bowl, leaving the cooking liquid in the pot, and cover the bowl with aluminum foil to keep warm.

9. Place the lettuce in the Instant Pot to cook in the mushroom liquid and lock the lid. Program to pressure cook for 0 minutes on high pressure.

10. Set a timer for 5 minutes. When it sounds, quick release any pressure, carefully remove the lid, and stir the lettuce.

11. On a large platter, arrange the lettuce around the perimeter. Place the cooked mushrooms on the lettuce and serve.

INGREDIENT TIP: I like big, thick shiitake mushrooms that have a design on the cap. If you have time, begin soaking them the night before. If you only soak them for 30 minutes, soak a few extra in case some need more soaking time. You can keep soaking them and set them aside for other recipes. One of my favorite condiments is oyster sauce and I use it for everything. For those who prefer a shellfish-free option or a vegan option, consider using a mushroom "oyster" sauce.

BROCCOLI WITH GARLIC

Broccoli stir-fried with garlic is such a simple and delicious recipe. Because broccoli cooks so fast in the Instant Pot, it's important to take it out when it's ready, 2 to 3 minutes after you put on the lid. If you have an Instant Pot glass lid, use it with the Sauté function. Otherwise, remember to switch to pressure cooking, then remove the broccoli before the Instant Pot seals.

SERVES 4

PREP TIME:
5 minutes

SAUTÉ:
5 minutes

PRESSURE BUILD:
3 minutes

PRESSURE COOK:
0 minutes, high

PRESSURE RELEASE:
Quick

TOTAL TIME:
13 minutes

1 teaspoon neutral oil

2 garlic cloves, chopped

¼ teaspoon salt (optional)

12 ounces fresh broccoli florets

½ cup vegetable broth or water

1. On the Instant Pot, select Sauté to preheat the pot. Once hot, pour in the oil and add the garlic. Stir-fry for 1 minute until fragrant.

2. Sprinkle the salt (if using) into the pot, add the broccoli, and stir-fry for 1 minute.

3. Pour in the broth and immediately lock the lid.

4. Program to pressure cook for 0 minutes on high pressure. The broccoli will finish as soon as the Instant Pot seals. If your Instant Pot requires a minimum of 1 minute for pressure cooking, set a timer for 3 minutes. When it sounds, quick release the pressure. Carefully remove the lid and stir. The broccoli is ready to serve.

PREP TIP: Cleanup for this recipe takes a few minutes and you can use the Instant Pot for another recipe. Or, steam an entrée first, then pour out the water and make this broccoli dish. Both dishes will still be hot and ready to eat at the same time. I also like to pressure cook hard-boiled eggs, corn on the cob, or artichokes while I prep other dishes, so I can use my Instant Pot to make two or three dishes in a row.

STEAMED MIXED VEGETABLES

I love eating mixed vegetables. It's like a bouquet of colors and flavors made with stir-fry vegetables that are crisp-tender when cooked correctly. I use carrots, broccoli florets, cauliflower florets, and zucchini but you can mix it up with mushrooms, bell peppers, snap peas, etc. Eat a rainbow of colors by using rainbow carrots, purple cauliflower, or bell peppers in a variety of colors. If you use a steamer basket, pressure cook for 0 minutes (or 1 minute and quick release when your Instant Pot seals). This recipe steams about 4 cups of seasoned vegetables using the pot-in-pot method (see page 5), so you can remove the bowl of vegetables, then use the Instant Pot to cook another dish.

SERVES 4

PREP TIME:
10 minutes

PRESSURE BUILD:
9 minutes

PRESSURE COOK:
1 minute, high

PRESSURE RELEASE:
Quick

TOTAL TIME:
20 minutes

½ cup water, plus 2 tablespoons
4 ounces fresh broccoli florets
4 ounces carrots, sliced
4 ounces cauliflower florets

4 ounces zucchini, sliced
1 teaspoon sesame oil (optional)
1 teaspoon light soy sauce (optional)

1. Pour ½ cup water into the Instant Pot and place a trivet inside. Pour the remaining 2 tablespoons of water into a 4-cup capacity pressure-safe bowl.

2. In a large bowl, combine the broccoli, carrots, cauliflower, zucchini, sesame oil (if using), and soy sauce (if using). Transfer the seasoned vegetables to the pressure-safe bowl. Place the bowl onto the trivet.

3. Lock the lid. Program to pressure cook for 1 minute on high pressure.

4. When the timer sounds, quick release the pressure and carefully remove the lid. The vegetables are ready to serve.

VARIATION: If you wanted to cook rice (see page 103) and these vegetables at the same time, put the rice and water into the pot, place a 2-inch-tall trivet into the pot, then tightly wrap the bowl of vegetables with aluminum foil and place it on the trivet. The trivet will elevate the vegetables away from direct heat and the foil will further insulate the vegetables from cooking too fast while the rice cooks (4 minutes at high pressure, 10-minute natural pressure release).

NAPA CABBAGE WITH MUNG BEAN VERMICELLI

Mung bean vermicelli looks like a hot dog bun–shaped bundle of dried white noodles, but when cooked, it's translucent. For that reason, mung bean vermicelli is also called glass noodles or Chinese vermicelli. It's a delicious ingredient in soups and braises and considered a low-glycemic-index food and an option for some special diets. There are many variations of this dish with julienned cabbage, or *mo qua* (fuzzy melon) cut into ½-inch sticks instead of napa cabbage. Other variations might include Chinese sausages or dried shrimp. I made this dish vegan by adding carrots and sweet onion for umami.

SERVES 6

PREP TIME:
10 minutes

SAUTÉ:
7 minutes

PRESSURE BUILD:
7 minutes

PRESSURE COOK:
1 minute, high

PRESSURE RELEASE:
Quick

TOTAL TIME:
25 minutes

2 bundles mung bean vermicelli
1 pound napa cabbage
1 teaspoon neutral oil
½ sweet onion, sliced
2 garlic cloves, chopped
2 carrots, sliced on the diagonal

1 cup vegetable broth or water
1 tablespoon light soy sauce
2 scallions, white and green parts, chopped

1. In a medium bowl, cover the mung bean vermicelli with water and soak for 5 minutes. Drain, halve the vermicelli, and set aside.

2. Cut the cabbage leaves into ½-inch sections through the stalk and 1-inch sections through the leaves (you should have 12 cups). Set aside.

3. Select Sauté to preheat the pot. Once hot, pour in the oil and add the onion and garlic. Stir-fry for 1 minute until fragrant.

4. Add the carrots and cabbage and stir-fry for 2 minutes until slightly softened.

5. Stir in the broth and soy sauce. Add the vermicelli and push it down halfway. Add the scallions.

6. Lock the lid. Program to pressure cook for 1 minute on high pressure. When the timer sounds, quick release the pressure.

7. Carefully remove the lid, then stir. The vegetables and vermicelli are ready to serve.

RED BRAISED CAULIFLOWER WITH ROAST PORK

This cooking method is like the red braise method for making pork belly (see page 66), using oil to melt and caramelize sugar. My mom was ahead of her time, cooking cauliflower like one would cook meat. My mom used to cook cauliflower this way with leftover roast pork for flavor. Buying roast pork can be hit or miss depending on which cut is available at the time of purchase. If the roast pork is tasty, there won't be much left over. This recipe simply uses up the so-so pieces for flavor. If you don't have roast pork, omit or use a Chinese sausage or cooked chicken. The cauliflower will be ready before the Instant Pot chimes, so you'll need to use another timer.

SERVES 4

PREP TIME:
5 minutes

SAUTÉ:
5 minutes

PRESSURE BUILD:
2 minutes

PRESSURE COOK:
0 minutes, high

PRESSURE RELEASE:
Quick

TOTAL TIME:
12 minutes

1 tablespoon neutral oil

2 tablespoons sugar

½ cup chopped roast pork

4 cups (12 ounces) fresh cauliflower florets

½ cup chicken broth or water

2 teaspoons light soy sauce or oyster sauce

1. On the Instant Pot, select Sauté. Pour in the oil and add the sugar while the pot is still cold. Cook for about 3 minutes, stirring continuously as the sugar starts to melt and the pot heats. Add the pork and stir-fry until it becomes a bit brown.

2. Add the cauliflower and stir-fry for 1 minute.

3. Pour in the broth and soy sauce and stir to loosen any food stuck to the pot.

4. Lock the lid. Program to pressure cook for 0 minutes (or 1 minute) on high pressure.

5. Set a timer for 2 minutes. When it sounds, quick release the pressure and carefully remove the lid.

6. Stir so the cauliflower pieces cook evenly in the residual heat.

KABOCHA SQUASH WITH FERMENTED BLACK BEANS AND GARLIC

Kabocha is a Japanese winter squash that is sweet and has a dark-green peel that is tender when cooked. My mom used to cook butternut squash this way with garlic and douchi (fermented black soybeans), which is also delicious. The sweetness of the squash and savoriness of the douchi and garlic are a great contrast. I prefer cooking with kabocha because it requires less work, since peeling a kabocha is optional and I cut off the rough brown parts of the squash but leave the green parts of the peel on.

SERVES 6

PREP TIME:
10 minutes

SAUTÉ:
5 minutes

PRESSURE BUILD:
7 minutes

PRESSURE COOK:
5 minutes, high

PRESSURE RELEASE:
Natural, 5 minutes

TOTAL TIME:
32 minutes

½ small kabocha squash

2 garlic cloves, peeled

1 tablespoon douchi, rinsed, or 1 tablespoon black bean sauce

2 teaspoons neutral oil

½ cup vegetable broth or water

2 teaspoons light soy sauce (omit if using black bean sauce)

1 teaspoon sugar

1. Use a cleaver or sharp chef's knife to peel away any rough brown spots from the kabocha's surface. Cut the kabocha into 2-inch pieces (you should have 6 to 8 cups) and set aside.

2. Coarsely chop the garlic. Place the douchi on the garlic and chop them together.

3. On the Instant Pot, select Sauté to preheat the pot. Once hot, pour in the oil and add the douchi and garlic. Stir-fry for 1 minute until fragrant.

4. Add the kabocha and stir-fry for 1 minute to coat the pieces. Select Cancel.

5. Pour in the broth, soy sauce, and sugar and stir to loosen any food stuck to the pot.

6. Lock the lid. Program to pressure cook for 5 minutes on high pressure.

7. When the timer sounds, let the pressure release naturally for 5 minutes, then quick release the remaining pressure.

8. Carefully remove the lid and stir the kabocha so the top pieces get coated with sauce.

SPICY GARLIC CHINESE EGGPLANT

Chinese eggplant has a sweet, mild flavor because it doesn't have as many seeds as regular eggplant. As a result, Chinese eggplant requires less prep to cook. Look for eggplants that are long and cucumber-shaped, that feel heavy for their size, and that are evenly purple without blemishes.

SERVES 4

PREP TIME:
10 minutes

SAUTÉ:
5 minutes

PRESSURE BUILD:
5 minutes

PRESSURE COOK:
1 minute, high

PRESSURE RELEASE:
Quick

TOTAL TIME:
21 minutes

2 large Chinese eggplants
2 teaspoons neutral oil
4 garlic cloves, chopped
1 (¼-inch) piece fresh
   ginger, minced
1 teaspoon sugar
½ teaspoon red pepper flakes
½ cup water
1 tablespoon light soy sauce
2 scallions, white and green
   parts, chopped
Cooked rice, for serving (optional)

1. Cut off and discard the stem end of the eggplants. Roll-cut the eggplant: Cut a 1½-inch piece on the diagonal, roll the eggplant a quarter turn, and cut on the diagonal again. Each piece should be about 1½ inches long and look like a triangle, thin on one side and thick on the other (you should have about 6 cups).

2. On the Instant Pot, select Sauté to preheat the pot. Once hot, pour in the oil and add the garlic, ginger, sugar, and red pepper flakes. Stir-fry for about 1 minute until fragrant.

3. Add the eggplant and stir-fry for 1 minute. Select Cancel.

4. Pour in the water and soy sauce to deglaze the pot, scraping up any browned bits from the bottom.

5. Lock the lid. Program to pressure cook for 1 minute on high pressure.

6. When the timer sounds, quick release the pressure. Carefully remove the lid and stir in the scallions. Serve as is, or with rice.

VARIATION: To make with pork, add 2 ounces of lean ground pork after step 3 and stir-fry until browned.

GREEN BEANS WITH SPICY MEAT SAUCE

One of my favorite Chinese restaurant dishes is Sichuan-style dry-fried string beans. If done correctly, the string beans are deep-fried until blistered but tender, then stir-fried in a spicy meat sauce. This Instant Pot adaptation steams green beans until crisp-tender, then calls for stir-frying with a spicy meat sauce until slightly smoky and charred.

SERVES 4

PREP TIME:
10 minutes

SAUTÉ:
7 minutes

PRESSURE BUILD:
5 minutes

PRESSURE COOK:
1 minute, high

PRESSURE RELEASE:
Quick

TOTAL TIME:
23 minutes

½ cup water

1 pound green beans, trimmed

1 tablespoon neutral oil

4 garlic cloves, minced

½ teaspoon red pepper flakes

1 tablespoon dried shrimp (optional)

2 ounces ground pork, or
  1 lap cheong (Chinese
  sausage), chopped

2 teaspoons light soy sauce

1. Pour the water into the Instant Pot and add the green beans.

2. Lock the lid. Program to pressure cook on high pressure for 1 minute.

3. When the timer sounds, quick release the pressure and carefully remove the lid. Drain the beans in a colander in the sink. Rinse and dry the liner before returning it to the base.

4. Select Sauté to preheat the pot. Once hot, pour in the oil and add the garlic, red pepper flakes, and dried shrimp (if using). Stir-fry for 1 minute until fragrant.

5. Add the ground pork and stir-fry for about 1 minute until the pork is brown.

6. Return the green beans to the pot and stir-fry for 1 minute until the pork is cooked through.

7. Stir in the soy sauce. Select Cancel and let the green beans sear in the residual heat without stirring for another minute. Gently stir the green beans before serving.

Gluten-Free   **Soy-Free**   **Vegan**

STEAMED WHITE RICE

Steamy, hot white rice is so satisfying when freshly cooked. The recipe cooks the rice at high pressure in a short time, which gets the job done. I have cooked long-grain white rice, which comes out fluffy, and medium-grain Calrose rice, which comes out sticky. You can reheat leftovers on a tall trivet while you cook a different dish or add some to soup to turn a simple bowl into a meal.

SERVES 4

PREP TIME:
15 minutes

PRESSURE BUILD:
10 minutes

PRESSURE COOK:
4 minutes, high

PRESSURE RELEASE:
Natural, 10 minutes

TOTAL TIME:
39 minutes

1½ cups white rice (your choice)   **1½ cups water**

1. In a medium bowl, rinse and drain the rice two times, then soak it in water for at least 10 minutes.

2. Drain the rice and pour it into the Instant Pot. Pour in the water.

3. Lock the lid. Program to pressure cook for 4 minutes on high pressure.

4. When the timer sounds, let the pressure release naturally for 10 minutes, then quick release any remaining pressure. Fluff the rice and serve.

VARIATION: Similar to cooking rice on the stovetop or in a rice cooker, there's a slower way to cook rice in the Instant Pot that will make soft rice. Either use the Instant Pot's default Rice setting or program it to pressure cook for 12 minutes on low pressure and release the pressure naturally for 10 minutes. You can also use the Instant Pot's Delay Cook feature, which allows the rice to soak longer, and the rice will be ready when you are. Brown rice needs more soaking time and more cooking time (20 minutes on high pressure in the pot followed by natural pressure release).

CHICKEN AND GARLIC SHALLOT RICE

This rice is usually served on the side with Hainan chicken. Packed with savory and aromatic flavors, this rice is so good, you can enjoy it as a side dish with any recipe in this book, especially Chicken Leg Quarters with Ginger-Scallion Sauce (page 76). While the chicken legs cool, strain and reserve the cooking liquid, and use ¾ cup of the cooking liquid plus ¾ cup of water instead of the chicken stock for the rice.

SERVES 4

PREP TIME:
15 minutes

SAUTÉ:
6 minutes

PRESSURE BUILD:
10 minutes

PRESSURE COOK:
12 minutes, low

PRESSURE RELEASE:
Natural, 10 minutes

TOTAL TIME:
53 minutes

1½ cups long-grain white rice
2 teaspoons neutral oil
1 shallot, chopped
2 garlic cloves, chopped

1½ cups Chicken Stock with Ginger (page 32)
½ teaspoon sesame oil (optional)

1. In a medium bowl, rinse and drain the rice two times, then soak it in water for at least 10 minutes.

2. On the Instant Pot, select Sauté and adjust the heat to high to preheat the pot. Once hot, pour in the oil and add the shallot. Stir-fry for about 2 minutes until soft.

3. Add the garlic and stir-fry for about 1 minute until fragrant.

4. Drain the rice, add the rice to the pot, and stir. Pour in the stock to deglaze the pot, scraping up any browned bits from the bottom.

5. Lock the lid. Program to pressure cook for 12 minutes on low pressure.

6. When the timer sounds, let the pressure release naturally for 10 minutes, then quick release any remaining pressure.

7. Carefully remove the lid. Drizzle in the sesame oil (if using) and fluff the rice.

8. Serve immediately, or transfer the rice to a serving bowl and cover with aluminum foil until ready to serve.

KABOCHA AND CHICKEN CONGEE

This recipe is a mashup inspired by a pumpkin and ginger dessert soup and by my desire to add vegetables to congee. Kabocha is slightly sweet, but the sweetness is enhanced by the savory chicken. This is a nice one-pot meal that's satisfying on a cold day. The kabocha peel is edible—it's only necessary to trim off the rough brown parts of the squash. If you can't find kabocha, try peeled butternut squash or sweet potatoes cut into large cubes.

SERVES 6

PREP:
20 minutes

**PRESSURE
BUILD:**
20 minutes

**PRESSURE
COOK:**
60 minutes,
high

**PRESSURE
RELEASE:**
Natural,
25 minutes

TOTAL TIME:
2 hours
5 minutes

1½ cups long-grain or jasmine white rice

8 cups Chicken Stock with Ginger (page 32)

4 cups cubed (2-inch pieces) kabocha

3 boneless, skinless chicken thighs

1 (½-inch) piece fresh ginger, thinly sliced

½ teaspoon salt

1. In a medium bowl, rinse and drain the rice two times. Pour the rice into the Instant Pot.

2. Pour in the stock and add the kabocha, chicken, ginger, and salt.

3. Lock the lid. Program to pressure cook for 60 minutes on high pressure.

4. When the timer sounds, let the pressure release naturally for 25 minutes.

5. Carefully remove the lid, stir, and serve in soup bowls.

VARIATION: I like eating rice porridge, but I find it more satisfying with some add-ins or toppings, which is the inspiration for this recipe. If you want to include more vegetables, stir in some thawed frozen peas when you remove the lid. Or, top your bowl with sautéed mushrooms, a fried egg, or shredded lettuce.

STICKY RICE WITH CHINESE SAUSAGES AND DRIED SHRIMP

Called *no mai fan*, but also known as *loh mai fan*, this Cantonese-style sticky rice is always a favorite side dish. It's very easy to make in the Instant Pot. The main ingredient is sweet rice, sometimes called sweet glutinous rice.

SERVES 6

PREP TIME:
15 minutes, plus 30 minutes to soak

SAUTÉ:
10 minutes

PRESSURE BUILD:
5 minutes

PRESSURE COOK:
12 minutes, low

PRESSURE RELEASE:
Natural, 10 minutes

TOTAL TIME:
1 hour 22 minutes

3 dried shiitake mushrooms

2 cups sweet glutinous rice

¼ cup dried shrimp

2 lap cheong (Chinese sausages), cut into ¼-inch slices

2 teaspoons neutral oil, divided

1 teaspoon sugar

1 teaspoon light soy sauce

1⅓ cups water

2 celery stalks, chopped

½ cup chopped scallions, white and green parts

¼ cup chopped fresh cilantro (optional)

1 tablespoon oyster sauce

1. Rinse the shiitake mushrooms, then cover them with water to soak for 30 minutes, or until soft. Drain. Remove and discard the stems. Dice the mushrooms.

2. Rinse and drain the rice two times, then soak it in water for 30 minutes. Drain.

3. Rinse the dried shrimp and cover them with water to soak for 5 minutes. Drain.

4. On the Instant Pot, select Sauté and adjust the heat to high. Place the lap cheong in the cold pot to render some of its fat.

5. When the pot is hot, pour in 1 teaspoon of oil and add the shrimp. Stir-fry for about 1 minute until the shrimp is fragrant and the sausage is sizzling.

6. Add the mushrooms and sugar. Stir-fry for 1 minute.

7. Select Cancel. Stir in the soy sauce and immediately transfer the sausage, shrimp, and mushrooms to a medium bowl.

8. Add the rice to the pot and stir to mix. Stir in the water to deglaze the pot, scraping up any browned bits from the bottom

9. Lock the lid. Program to pressure cook on low pressure for 12 minutes.

10. When the timer sounds, let the pressure release naturally for 10 minutes, then quick release the remaining pressure.

11. Carefully remove the lid and add the sausage mixture, celery, scallions, and cilantro (if using).

12. Lock the lid. Allow the residual heat to steam the celery and herbs for 5 minutes.

13. Remove the lid, add the oyster sauce, and fold the sausage and other ingredients into the rice. The rice is ready to serve.

PREP TIP: Many of the ingredients in this recipe can be prepped ahead to save time. Soak the mushrooms and rice overnight in the refrigerator. Prepare the lap cheong, celery, scallions, and cilantro and wrap and refrigerate. When you are ready to cook, drain the rice and chop the mushrooms.

RICE CONGEE TWO WAYS: PLAIN OR CHICKEN

Plain rice congee is often served for breakfast with a variety of toppings to personalize your bowl. I like fresh ingredients, such as shredded iceberg lettuce, cilantro, or scallion, and some savory crunchy bits like fried shallot, fried onion, or toasted sesame seeds. More traditional ingredients might include roasted peanuts, minced salted and preserved turnips, and sliced *youtiao* (Chinese doughnut sticks). My children like very thick congee, so I use 8 cups of water for this recipe. Most people like a rice-to-water ratio of 1:6 (9 cups for this recipe) and up to a 1:8 ratio (12 cups for this recipe). If I'm serving congee for lunch or dinner, I make it with chicken and thinly sliced fresh ginger. If I'm serving congee for breakfast, I cook it right before I go to sleep, then proceed with step 5 in the morning. The Instant Pot will keep your congee warm for 10 hours. If it's cold, use the Saute function to warm it for a few minutes, until it bubbles.

SERVES 6

PREP TIME:
10 minutes

PRESSURE BUILD:
30 minutes

PRESSURE COOK:
60 minutes, high

PRESSURE RELEASE:
Natural, 25 minutes

TOTAL TIME:
2 hours 5 minutes

FOR THE CONGEE

1½ cups long-grain or jasmine white rice

8 to 12 cups water or Chicken Stock with Ginger (page 32)

6 boneless, skinless chicken thighs (optional)

1 (½-inch) piece fresh ginger, thinly sliced

½ teaspoon salt

FOR SERVING
(CHOOSE 2 OR MORE ITEMS)

¼ head iceberg lettuce, thinly sliced

2 cups chopped cooked vegetables of choice

½ cup chopped fresh cilantro

½ cup thinly sliced scallion, white and green parts

¼ cup fried onions

¼ cup fried shallots

TO MAKE THE CONGEE

1. In a medium bowl, rinse and drain the rice two times.

2. In the Instant Pot, combine the rice, water, chicken (if using), ginger, and salt.

3. Lock the lid. Program to pressure cook on high pressure for 60 minutes.

4. When the timer sounds, let the pressure release naturally for 25 minutes.

5. Carefully remove the lid. Stir the congee until it's evenly mixed.

TO SERVE THE CONGEE

6. Serve the congee topped as desired.

VARIATION: A third variation is to add thinly sliced fish fillets to plain congee. Cook plain congee (without chicken) as directed. Select 8 ounces of your favorite white fish fillet and remove any bones. Cut the fillet into ¼-inch slices, select Sauté at step 5, stir the congee, then gently stir in the fish and cook for 4 to 5 minutes until the congee bubbles. For more topping ideas, see the tip in the Kabocha and Chicken Congee, page 105.

MEASUREMENT CONVERSIONS

VOLUME EQUIVALENTS	U.S. STANDARD	U.S. STANDARD (OUNCES)	METRIC (APPROXIMATE)
LIQUID	2 tablespoons	1 fl. oz.	30 mL
	¼ cup	2 fl. oz.	60 mL
	½ cup	4 fl. oz.	120 mL
	1 cup	8 fl. oz.	240 mL
	1½ cups	12 fl. oz.	355 mL
	2 cups or 1 pint	16 fl. oz.	475 mL
	4 cups or 1 quart	32 fl. oz.	1 L
	1 gallon	128 fl. oz.	4 L
DRY	⅛ teaspoon		0.5 mL
	¼ teaspoon		1 mL
	½ teaspoon		2 mL
	¾ teaspoon		4 mL
	1 teaspoon		5 mL
	1 tablespoon		15 mL
	¼ cup		59 mL
	⅓ cup		79 mL
	½ cup		118 mL
	⅔ cup		156 mL
	¾ cup		177 mL
	1 cup		235 mL
	2 cups or 1 pint		475 mL
	3 cups		700 mL
	4 cups or 1 quart		1 L
	½ gallon		2 L
	1 gallon		4 L

OVEN TEMPERATURES

FAHRENHEIT	CELSIUS (APPROXIMATE)
250°F	120°C
300°F	150°C
325°F	165°C
350°F	180°C
375°F	190°C
400°F	200°C
425°F	220°C
450°F	230°C

WEIGHT EQUIVALENTS

U.S. STANDARD	METRIC (APPROXIMATE)
½ ounce	15 g
1 ounce	30 g
2 ounces	60 g
4 ounces	115 g
8 ounces	225 g
12 ounces	340 g
16 ounces or 1 pound	455 g

RESOURCES

You'll find many of the fresh and shelf-stable ingredients listed in the recipes at your local supermarket or Asian grocery store. Support your local Asian markets whenever possible. The following are some online resources for ingredients, if they aren't available locally.

99 Ranch Market has local stores that sell fresh produce, meats, and shelf-stable items. Online orders for shelf-stable products are shipped to your home.
99ranch.com

My Asian Store distributes shelf-stable Asian groceries. They have 15+ years of experience shipping shelf-stable products within the continental US.
MyAsianStore.com

Weee sells a wide range of Asian groceries, including fresh produce and meats. Check their list of locations for local fresh deliveries. Otherwise they ship shelf-stable ingredients.
SayWeee.com

The Mala Market is known for its collection of Sichuan spices and other essential Chinese cooking ingredients.
TheMalaMarket.com

INDEX

Acknowledgments

Many thanks to Jimmy, Matthew, and Brandon for their unconditional love and support while I wrote this cookbook and for being willing taste testers. I'm thankful for my loving mother and my late father, who taught me everything I know about cooking and appreciating Chinese food.

I'm thankful for Jenny, Homa, and all the FABlogCon friends who loved my idea to share nut-free Asian recipes. Thank you to all of my *Nut Free Wok* readers for reading my blog over the years and for your kind feedback. I'm always thinking of you. Thank you to Robin and Terri for your advice and help. Thank you to Tamara, Jennifer, Theresa, and Kristin for your frequent check-ins.

I am grateful to the editors at Callisto Media for their ideas and support to write this book and special thanks to my amazing editor, Anna Pulley, for her kind encouragement throughout the process.

About the Author

Sharon Wong is a mom and food allergy advocate who lives in the San Francisco Bay Area with her husband and two college-age sons. She is a graduate of UC Berkeley, where she studied molecular biology and English literature, and went on to earn her master's in education at UCLA. She was an elementary school computer teacher before becoming a mom. She founded her blog, *Nut Free Wok*, in 2013 and uses her background in science, English, education, and technology to help families with food allergies enjoy Asian food and to advocate for food allergy awareness, legislation, and treatment. She has been featured on *NBC Asian America*, was recognized as a top blogger by Healthline, and has been invited to share cooking demonstrations at conferences and events. Her favorite foods are dim sum and durian. You can find more recipes and information on NutFreeWok.com and find Sharon on social media @NutFreeWok.